Health Psychology in Clinical Practice

Health Psychology in Clinical Practice provides a collection of first-hand accounts from several of the most established and experienced clinically working Health Psychologists in the UK, explaining what they do, how they do it and why their work is important.

In recent years, health psychologists have come into their own in being able to provide high-quality, evidence-based, clinical support for patients by utilising relevant therapies. Trainees and would-be clinical practitioners in the health psychology community are keen to learn more about this aspect of their craft, and this book provides a valuable source of information they can turn to – unlike the vast majority of literature on clinical practice in psychology, written by clinical psychologists, which is mostly of tangential relevance to a health psychologist. As a compilation, the first-hand accounts within *Health Psychology in Clinical Practice* provide a guide that will help define what clinical health psychology is and should be for a decade or more.

This book is an essential resource as a crucial snapshot of practice in the discipline in the UK and will additionally support trainees and those seeking a career in health psychology centred on practice rather than research or teaching.

Mark J. Forshaw is subject leader in Health and Applied Psychology at Liverpool John Moores University, UK. An international expert in psychology training, he runs a professional doctorate in Health Psychology. He is a practitioner and supervisor of practitioners, and the author of many papers and books in his field.

'This book is an invaluable and comprehensive resource for trainees, supervisors and practitioners. It provides expert accounts of the lived experience of becoming a health psychologist, whilst also presenting rich insights into assessment and formulation, clinical supervision, the setting up of health psychology services and the application of health psychology to a range of clinical settings. A must read for aspiring and current health psychologists.'

Dr Lynne Dunwoody, *Lecturer in Health Psychology, University of Ulster, and Chair, Partnership & Accreditation Committee of the British Psychological Society, UK*

'A useful, engaging, and informative edited text where the authors share their real-life experiences of health psychology training and practice, including some of the opportunities and challenges. The reader gets a clear view of the diverse skills necessary to be an effective health psychologist, and the text will be invaluable to health psychology trainees and those who teach health psychology students, particularly at postgraduate level.'

Professor Sarah Grogan, *Emeritus Professor, Manchester Metropolitan University, UK*

Health Psychology in Clinical Practice

Edited by
Mark J. Forshaw

LONDON AND NEW YORK

First published 2022
by Routledge
2 Park Square, Milton Park, Abingdon, Oxon OX14 4RN

and by Routledge
605 Third Avenue, New York, NY 10158

Routledge is an imprint of the Taylor & Francis Group, an informa business

© 2022 selection and editorial matter, Mark J. Forshaw; individual chapters, the contributors

The right of Mark J. Forshaw to be identified as the author of the editorial material, and of the authors for their individual chapters, has been asserted in accordance with sections 77 and 78 of the Copyright, Designs and Patents Act 1988.

All rights reserved. No part of this book may be reprinted or reproduced or utilised in any form or by any electronic, mechanical, or other means, now known or hereafter invented, including photocopying and recording, or in any information storage or retrieval system, without permission in writing from the publishers.

Trademark notice: Product or corporate names may be trademarks or registered trademarks, and are used only for identification and explanation without intent to infringe.

British Library Cataloguing-in-Publication Data
A catalogue record for this book is available from the British Library

Library of Congress Cataloging-in-Publication Data
Names: Forshaw, Mark, editor.
Title: Health psychology in clinical practice / edited by Mark J. Forshaw.
Description: Milton Park, Abingdon, Oxon ; New York, NY : Routledge, 2022. | Includes bibliographical references and index.
Identifiers: LCCN 2021023448 (print) | LCCN 2021023449 (ebook) | ISBN 9780367637330 (hardback) | ISBN 9780367637316 (paperback) | ISBN 9781003120469 (ebook)
Subjects: LCSH: Clinical health psychology.
Classification: LCC R726.7 H43358 2022 (print) | LCC R726.7 (ebook) | DDC 616.001/9--dc23
LC record available at https://lccn.loc.gov/2021023448
LC ebook record available at https://lccn.loc.gov/2021023449

ISBN: 978-0-367-63733-0 (hbk)
ISBN: 978-0-367-63731-6 (pbk)
ISBN: 978-1-003-12046-9 (ebk)

DOI: 10.4324/9781003120469

Typeset in Baskerville
by Taylor & Francis Books

Contents

List of illustrations vii
Acknowledgements ix
List of contributors xii

Introduction 1
MARK J. FORSHAW

1 Supporting people to live with and manage long-term physical health conditions 3
KATE HAMILTON-WEST

2 Health Psychology in an NHS pain management service 19
LAURA HISSEY

3 The twists and turns into Health Psychology 31
NEESHA PATEL

4 Delivering an NHS Health Psychology service for patients with eye cancer 42
LAURA HOPE-STONE

5 A spectrum of applied Health Psychology: Across public health and healthcare practice 60
LISA NEWSON

6 Beating your imposter syndrome to become a practitioner Health Psychologist 75
KOULA ASIMAKOPOULOU

| 7 | Health Psychology in a clinical setting: How it works for me | 87 |

JENNIFER PULMAN

| 8 | Assessment in Health Psychology clinical practice | 98 |

ELEANOR BULL AND HANNAH DALE

| 9 | Formulation in Health Psychology clinical practice | 117 |

HANNAH DALE AND ELEANOR BULL

Afterword 159

MARK J. FORSHAW

Index 161

Illustrations

Figures

1.1	Interrelationships between Health Psychology roles	4
1.2	Questions to consider for developing a career in health psychology	6
1.3	Theoretical frameworks	8
1.4	Communicating the concept of self-efficacy through origami	11
1.5	Five key imperatives for Health Psychologists providing direct patient care	12
1.6	Health Psychology practice sits at the interface between science, person and context	14
4.1	Case study: assessment and case formulation	47
4.2	Social-cognitive transition model of adjustment	50
7.1	Process of client work	93
9.1	CBT five areas formulation example	124
9.2	Combined five areas and five Ps formulation example	128
9.3	Acceptance and Commitment Therapy (ACT) formulation example	130
9.4	Common Sense Model (CSM) formulation example	132
9.5	Transdiagnostic model of adjustment formulation example	134
9.6	Motivation, Action Prompts (MAP) model formulation example	136
9.7	Theoretical Domains Framework (TDF) and Capability, Opportunity, Motivation - Behaviour (COM-B) integrated formulation example	139
9.8	Transtheoretical model (TTM) formulation example	147
9.9	Stepped care model of psychological interventions in health psychology clinical practice	154

List of illustrations

Tables

9.1	ABC functional analysis example	122
9.2	Formulation tools rated against four considerations for use in clinical practice	125

Boxes

8.1	Case vignette: Anita	101
8.2	Engaging clients in a Health Psychology assessment	102
8.3	Exploring health symptoms and beliefs	106
8.4.	Broad areas of measurement relevant to Health Psychology, including examples of specific measurement tools	108
8.5	Discussing information from within standardised measures	109
9.1	Case vignette: Anita	119
9.2	Case vignette: John	120
9.3	Case vignette: Sinead	120

Acknowledgements

I would like to thank all of the authors of the chapters in this book, who took on my challenge and helped to make this happen. I never fail to be impressed by them and what they do. I am proud of them and honoured to know them.

Mark J. Forshaw

I would like to acknowledge the contributions of my research collaborators, colleagues, students, patients, participants and funders without whom these projects would not have been possible.

Kate Hamilton-West

I would like to thank Dr Mark Forshaw for inviting me to write my chapter; it has certainly taken me back in time and made me re-live some of the tear-jerking moments of my life as well as feel gratitude for my achievements. It has also given me the much-needed opportunity to reflect on my career journey to date, and hope that sharing my story will help inspire others too.

Neesha Patel

I would like to thank Peter Salmon, for all his guidance, and Jeff and James Hill, for all their love and support.

Laura Hope-Stone

To all the individuals whom I have had the opportunity to manage and work alongside, have been led by or observed their leadership, I would like to say thank you for your inspiration, guidance and feedback. Without the support from my peers, colleagues and stakeholders, I would not be the Health Psychologist I am today, and I want to say thank you especially to those who worked with me in NHS Cheshire and Wirral Partnership NHS Foundation Trust; NHS Knowsley; Liverpool City Council; Knowsley

x   *Acknowledgements*

Council – Kerri M., Ruth F., Liz S., Julie T., Chris Mc., Chris O. My initial inspiration for academic research comes from Professor Marion Hetherington, my undergraduate supervisor and line manager at the University of Liverpool. I want to thank Dr Rachel Povey and Dr Mark Forshaw for my guidance and supervision as a Health Psychologist in Training whilst completing my doctorate studies at Staffordshire University and all those Health Psychologists I have worked with and learnt from. I have many academic colleagues who continue to offer guidance and inspiration, motivating my ongoing working practice; with special thanks to, Prof. Zoe Knowles, Dr Julie Abayomi and Dr Mark Forshaw. I thoroughly enjoy learning from my trainees and students who aspire to become Health Psychologists, and I thank you for the shared learning and new evidence we have created together, Dr Tasneem Patel, Dr Ishfaq Vaja, Dr Ben Gibson, Dr Nicola Sides, Dr Michael Owens, Dr Ng Kheng Ban, and many other students. I thank my parents for their continuous belief, encouragement and for giving me the opportunity to be the first to go university and get a degree (or three).

I want to thank my husband, Lee; he has put up with me all through my career development, since A levels he has witnessed it all: the highs, the lows and the bits in the middle. He has supported me with love and patience and offered a listening ear when I was stressed, frustrated or overly excited about a new project idea. Finally, this chapter is for my two girls, Seren aged six and Freya aged two (but almost three), both of whom fill my life with love, fun and joy; I hope they will follow their dreams and create a future career and life full of interest and excitement.

Lisa Newson

I would like to thank Dr Mark Forshaw for inviting me to contribute to this much needed book, and for supporting me all throughout my health psychology journey and private clinical career. Without his support I simply would not be in a position to write this chapter. I would also like to thank all the people who been involved in my educational pathway, my university lecturers and placement collaborators and every one of my colleagues from all my early career places of work. I would like to thank my family for all their continued support and encouragement, my partner Stephen for always being positively encouraging and supportive and my son Jack for being there when I come home from clinic. Most of all I want to thank all of the clients I have worked alongside, for trusting me with their deepest, most personal experiences. This is my greatest honour.

Jennifer Pulman

We wish to thank Professor Rona Moss-Morris for her excellent guest speaker session at the Manchester Health Psychology Skills Practice Group which influenced our thinking on this topic. Thank you to Professor Rona Moss-Morris, Dr Susan Carroll and Dr Zoe Moon for advice on the manuscripts and sharing their forthcoming paper. Thank you to the NHS Education for Scotland Trainee Health psychologists who have been 'guinea-pigs' for many of the formulation tools and provided useful feedback. We'd also like to thank Dr Alyssa Lee, Holly Martin-Smith and Dr Claire Hallas for helpful comments on earlier versions of these chapters.

Eleanor Bull and Hannah Dale

List of contributors

Dr Koula Asimakopoulou is the founder of The Mind Umbrella. A chartered psychologist with the British Psychological Society (BPS) and a HCPC-registered psychologist, Koula was awarded her doctorate (PhD) in Health Psychology in 2001 and has since undertaken further training to include qualifications in cognitive behaviour therapy (CBT), third wave CBT therapies and motivational interviewing. Koula is a qualified psychometric test assessor trained to administer, interpret and give people feedback on personality and ability (intelligence) tests. In addition to being the founder of The Mind Umbrella, Koula holds an academic position at King's College London, based at Guy's Hospital. Koula's work focuses on helping people take on behaviour change, deal with stressors, fears and phobias as well as supporting them in living with chronic conditions. Koula is one of three psychologists who set up and delivered the first ever NHS health psychology service designed to help people combat their fear of the dentist at Guy's Hospital, London.

Dr Eleanor Bull is a HCPC-registered Health Psychologist and BABCP-accredited cognitive behavioural therapist. Eleanor is the current practice lead for the British Psychological Society's Division of Health Psychology committee. As a practitioner health psychologist, Eleanor has worked within public health, NHS primary care, sexual health, HIV, diabetes and acute and chronic pain NHS secondary care multi-disciplinary teams as well as within a private online CBT service. In her academic role, Eleanor currently directs a BPS-accredited MSc Health Psychology programme, conducts applied health behaviour change research and supervisees Stage 2 health psychology trainees.

Dr Hannah Dale is a HCPC-registered health psychologist and a practitioner member of the Faculty of Public Health. She holds a PhD in clinical health psychology from the University of St Andrews and has over a decade of experience as a practitioner psychologist in the NHS. Her work has spanned individual-, group- and community-level interventions within psychology and public health, including working in oncology, blood-borne virus services, paediatric psychology, team-based GP practices, and drug and alcohol recovery services. Hannah also leads on the health psychology training programme in NHS Education for Scotland, providing supervision and training to health psychology trainees.

Dr Mark J. Forshaw is subject leader in Health and Applied Psychology in the School of Psychology at Liverpool John Moores University. He is the author and editor of a large number of books and papers, and is a practitioner Health Psychologist, an academic and a manager. He has previously served as a trustee of the British Psychological Society and president of the Institute of Health Promotion & Education. He is also the director of the Crisis & Pandemic Interest Group, based in Liverpool but with members across the globe.

Professor Kate Hamilton-West is a chartered psychologist, HCPC-registered Health Psychologist and professor of Health Psychology specialising in applying behavioural science to improve care and support for people living with long-term conditions. Her work has included developing, implementing and evaluating interventions to improve outcomes for people with arthritis, diabetes, heart disease, COPD, multiple sclerosis, stroke, depression, anxiety disorders and physical disabilities, as well as training interventions for a range of HCPs. She also developed and led an NHS Diabetes Psychology Service. Kate works for a global company specialising in Human Data Science and has an academic base at the University of Kent.

Dr Laura Hissey is a HCPC-registered Health Psychologist who specialises in pain management. The psychology lead for an NHS Pain Service in the West Midlands, she undertakes specialist assessments of complex cases and delivers face-to-face psychology interventions to support people to manage long-term pain conditions and improve general well-being. She has a background in working with people with long-term conditions and in addition to her pain specialism has worked clinically within cardiac rehabilitation and cardiovascular disease prevention services. She has also held consultancy roles within the local Public Health Directorate, as well as at The Department of Health & Public Health England where she provided psychological insights on national and local behaviour change programmes.

Laura Hope-Stone is a chartered Health Psychologist and HCPC-registered practitioner psychologist. After an extensive career in oncology nursing she trained as a Health Psychologist. Since 2010 she has provided a Health Psychology service for patients with ocular tumours at the Liverpool Ocular Oncology Centre at Liverpool University Hospitals NHS Foundation Trust. She is a Health Psychology Fellow in Oncology and clinical lecturer at the University of Liverpool. Laura's contact with patients is invaluable in ensuring

xiv List of contributors

patients' perspectives are integral to the psychological research programme, which includes: predictors of distress; patient reported outcomes; decision making; and coping with uncertainty in patients with ocular tumours.

Dr Lisa Newson is a reader in applied Health Psychology who has varied experience as a chartered Health Psychologist, and HCPC registered practitioner psychologist. She is a proud innovator of Health Psychology and has experience across the full spectrum of application within academia and healthcare practice. Dr Newson's expertise influences health prevention, overlapping with public health, and is applied directly to the management of long-term conditions. Her previous experience within the NHS, as a clinical practitioner, within public health commissioning and management, and as an applied researcher through academic-health collaborations, helps her bridge the 'knowledge-language gap' and add value between the ambitions and needs of academia and those working within healthcare.

Dr Neesha Patel is a clinical lead and Health Psychologist working at MoreLife Specialist Adult Weight Management Service in Greater Manchester. Neesha qualified as a Health Psychologist in 2014 and has worked in specialist weight management for over four years. She has specific expertise in the psychological aspects of obesity and diabetes management and specialises in helping people to understand the connection between emotions, eating behaviours and weight management. Neesha is extremely passionate about helping people to change their behaviour to lose weight and adopt a healthy lifestyle using psychological techniques.

Dr Jennifer Pulman is a registered Health Psychologist who has been providing psychological therapies since qualifying from Staffordshire University in 2014. She began working privately primarily with adults suffering with mental health difficulties and takes an individualised approach to therapy, often implementing a compassion focused therapy approach throughout much of her work. She also offers couples therapy to partners struggling with their romantic relationships, primarily using the Gottman therapeutic and interventional approach.

Introduction

Mark J. Forshaw

Health Psychology is evolving. It's only natural. The healthcare landscape changes continuously, and Health Psychologists must adapt and survive. Since it was first established as a defined discipline in the UK, this has been the way of things. It is mostly through small changes, rather than cataclysmic events: minor additions to the training curriculum, amendments to regulations, the incorporation of new theories, the banishment of older ones that no longer serve their purposes because the science doesn't support them any longer, and the advent of a new regulator with their own set of standards.

We have changed in the context of our kindred disciplines also evolving, particularly clinical, counselling and sport and exercise psychology. We have changed because people come and go, their influence ebbing and flowing, waxing and waning. Today's important committee on this and that is tomorrow's footnote in history, and that's no bad thing. In the UK, we are starting to be able to talk about *generations* of psychologists who have made their mark on the Health Psychology walk of fame.

Health Psychologists remain a broad church, not only spanning a vast range of areas of interest, with very few stones unturned where physical health meets human behaviour. They are also increasingly working in diverse environments, including, I am proud to say, *clinical* ones. We began by convincing others of our worth, of our unique contribution to clinical practice, and we are almost at the end of that phase. Apart from the cries of a few vestigial dinosaurs from earlier stages of evolution, almost no one would say that Health Psychology isn't needed in practice. It is, and it's here to stay. This book aims to show just that.

The writers of the chapters in this book show what it means to be a Health Psychologist in clinical practice. They are the pioneers, and we are rightly proud of them, and those like them, making a difference to the lives of patients and other stakeholders, plying evidence-based and evidence-informed solutions wherever they are needed and relevant.

DOI: 10.4324/9781003120469-1

Make no mistake: healthcare needs Health Psychologists. In the UK, the National Health Service needs Health Psychologists, and the much-beloved benign behemoth is waking up to that. The public needs Health Psychologists. Universities need Health Psychologists too, the practitioner type more than ever as we strive to enrich teaching with real-world examples. Theory and Practice are the twins who founded our modern discipline. Each feels empty without the other.

This book celebrates how far our particular trains have travelled, and the people who laid the tracks, who sell the tickets, and drive the locomotives. Progress has been rapid, fascinating, exciting, and holds so much promise yet.

It isn't like it was when I was a boy. Nobody ever said it should be. I like to think that it's much better.

1 Supporting people to live with and manage long-term physical health conditions

Kate Hamilton-West

This chapter provides a personal account of my experience as a Health Psychologist specialising in improving care and support for people with long-term physical health conditions (LTCs). I begin by considering how direct patient care fits with other aspects of my work, before going on to describe the approach I have taken to supporting patients with LTCs. I then reflect on some of the opportunities and challenges for Health Psychologists involved in direct patient care and suggest some future directions for Health Psychology practice.

How direct patient care fits with other aspects of my work as a Health Psychologist

> Health Psychology is the aggregate of the specific educational, scientific, and professional contributions of the discipline of psychology to the promotion and maintenance of health, the prevention and treatment of illness, the identification of etiologic and diagnostic correlates of health, illness, and related dysfunction and to the analysis and improvement of the health care system and health policy formation.
>
> (Matarazzo, 1982, p. 4)

As a professor of Health Psychology and HCPC (Health and Care Professions Council) registered Health Psychologist, my work has encompassed research, teaching and supervisory roles, along with service development, delivery and leadership, consultancy, and direct patient care. This has included for example, directing MSc programmes in Health Psychology and applied health research, supervising and examining PhD and professional doctorate students, developing and delivering training for health professionals supporting people with LTCs (e.g. Hamilton-West et al., 2018), developing behavioural science informed curricula for medical students (Hamilton-West, 2018b), developing and evaluating interventions to support self-management of

DOI: 10.4324/9781003120469-2

4 Kate Hamilton-West

diabetes (e.g. Hamilton-West et al., 2013) and enhancing self-efficacy in carers of children with disabilities (e.g. Hotham et al., 2017), developing and leading an NHS diabetes psychology service (Hamilton-West et al., 2014), working directly with people living with comorbid mental and physical health conditions (Hamilton-West, 2016), establishing and leading a regional Health Psychology network, acting as practitioner chair for the BPS Division of Health Psychology and as health psychology lead and Kent academic lead for the NIHR Research Design Service South East (part of the National Institute for Health Research).

These roles are very much interconnected. For example, knowledge of Health Psychology research and theory (maintained via research and teaching roles) feeds in to the development of services and interventions (delivered at one-to-one or group level), while knowledge of 'what works in practice' (developed via direct patient care and service development/ leadership) is fed back to refine theory and extend the evidence-base (e.g. via publications, conference presentations and training workshops). These interrelationships are illustrated in Figure 1.1 (below).

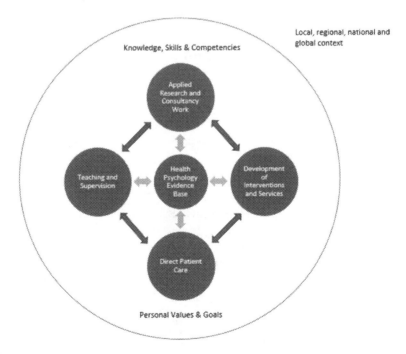

Figure 1.1 Interrelationships between Health Psychology roles

The outer circle (above) illustrates some of the factors that shape our work as Health Psychologists. For example, working as a Health Psychologist necessitates knowledge, skills and competencies relevant to the role (e.g. specific psychological therapies, or research methods), knowledge of adjacent disciplines and roles (e.g. health services research, behavioural and social sciences, other healthcare professions), awareness of relevant regulatory, professional and ethical frameworks (e.g. British Psychological Society, Health and Care Professions Council, NHS Health Research Authority) and understanding of the sector/context (e.g. NHS, Public Health, Higher Education). Ongoing work (e.g. CPD training, supervised practice, active engagement with professional bodies) is needed to ensure that these remain up to date.

While knowledge, skills and competencies represent *what* we need to know to work as Health Psychologists, personal values and goals explain *why* we do this work. For example, personal values might include a commitment to scientific integrity, or equality, diversity and inclusivity, while goals might include advancing disciplinary knowledge, or improving quality of life for people living with LTCs. Personal values and goals provide direction and meaning. It is possible to work towards these in various ways. For example, improving quality of life for people with LTCs may be achieved via direct patient care, by development of interventions and services, by training and supervising health professionals, or by conducting research that advances the underlying evidence-base. As such, the roles illustrated in Figure 1.1 can also be considered as pathways for translating Health Psychology research and methods into real world impact.

Beyond this circle are factors relating to the local, regional, national and global context. These include for example, global health challenges, government policy pertaining to health and social care, regional healthcare priorities and local health and wellbeing initiatives. These factors shape our work as Health Psychologists in various ways, such as by influencing the focus or availability of funding, raising awareness of issues relevant to our work (such as high levels of unmet psychological needs in people with LTCs), or providing opportunities to develop and implement interventions and services. We can also influence these agendas – for example, by disseminating research findings and examples of evidence-based practice, contributing to national consultations, working with local authority public health teams, or NHS clinical commissioning groups, or serving on relevant committees and advisory groups (e.g. for research funders, professional membership bodies, NHS Trusts, or national Government). Essentially, all of these examples involve sharing our expertise as Health Psychologists with relevant partners and stakeholders. To do so effectively, we need to build relationships beyond our own profession, identify

6 *Kate Hamilton-West*

opportunities to apply our knowledge and skills, communicate Health Psychology research and theory clearly (in terms that make sense to a range of specialist and non-specialist audiences) and act as 'ambassadors' for our profession – demonstrating the positive contributions Health Psychologists can make and the importance of incorporating Health Psychology perspectives. Working closely with partners and stakeholders also enables us to learn from others (e.g. patients, service users, carers, clinicians, service providers, commissioners and policy makers), ensuring that the work we do has 'real world' relevance and impact.

Supporting people living with long-term conditions

> Psychologists who provide healthcare services engage in evidence-based practice that is patient-centered, culturally competent, effective, and informed by population-based data. They are skilled in collaboration with other health professionals and demonstrate a commitment to lifelong learning and continuous quality improvement in their practice. They are grounded in psychological science and integrate knowledge from other areas such as biology and sociology into their practices as appropriate. They are not only critical consumers of psychological research, but able to conduct scientific research, especially practice-based outcomes research and program evaluation.
> (HSPEC, 2013, p. 1)

Working clinically as a Health Psychologist involves adopting approaches which are evidence-based and appropriately tailored to the individual and context, drawing on relevant research and theory. My own clinical work

---

Goals – What do you want to achieve in your work as a Health Psychologist?

Values – Why do you do this work? What makes it personally meaningful and rewarding?

Roles/Pathways – How can you work towards these values and goals through your current role? Are there other pathways you could explore?

Knowledge, skills and competencies – How does your training as a Health Psychologist equip you to work towards these goals? How can you continue to develop your knowledge, skills and competencies?

Context – How do your interests and goals as a Health Psychologist relate to local/regional/national/global healthcare priorities? Are there particular challenges/initiatives you could contribute to as a health psychologist?

Partners and stakeholders – Are there other individuals/groups/organisations with an interest in the same issues/challenges? How could you develop relationships with these?

Figure 1.2 Questions to consider for developing a career in health psychology

has mainly focused on supporting people living with LTCs, often in the context of reduced psychological wellbeing, including diagnosable mental health conditions. I draw from a wide evidence-base including epidemiological studies examining prevalence of psychological co-morbidities in people with LTCs (e.g. Katon, 2011), ethnographic research on patient experience of self-management (e.g. Hinder & Greenhalgh, 2012), research on predictors of 'adherence' (e.g. Delamater, 2006) and studies examining the effectiveness of psychological interventions for people with LTCs (e.g. Anderson & Ozakinci, 2018), as well as NICE guidance and reports by charities and government bodies (e.g. The Kings Fund, The Health Foundation, NHS England).

Theoretical frameworks I have found particularly useful in this context are the Common-Sense Model of Illness Representations (CSM; Leventhal et al., 1992) and Social Cognitive Theory (SCT; Bandura 1977). The former helps to explain how individuals make sense of and cope with their condition, while the latter explains how to help people develop confidence in their ability to carry out behaviours necessary for self-management (e.g. making changes to diet, physical activity, monitoring symptoms, or taking medicines). These models are can be used to guide direct patient care, to design interventions for people with LTCs and to train other health professionals to deliver patient-centred care (see Figure 1.3).

In terms of therapeutic approaches, I have found acceptance and commitment therapy (ACT) particularly helpful for supporting people to manage the wide-ranging impacts of chronic illness. ACT incorporates training in mindfulness and acceptance strategies (to improve management of negative thoughts, feelings and physical sensations, including illness symptoms and pain) and a focus on working towards goals and values in the face of difficulties (e.g. Brassington et al., 2016). This is important for people with LTCs since health problems often place constraints on daily living and interfere with valued goals. In addition, cognitive behavioural interventions (drawn from cognitive behavioural therapy; CBT) and motivational interventions (drawn from motivational interviewing; MI) can be used to support self-management by helping people to develop routines that are realistic and work for them over the long-term (see Hamilton-West et al., 2013).

Opportunities and challenges for Health Psychologists involved in direct patient care

As noted above, Health Psychologists have a broad skill set and are therefore equipped to work in a range of roles. While this is certainly a strength of the Health Psychology training pathway, it also presents a

8 Kate Hamilton-West

Social Cognitive Theory

According to social cognitive theory (SCT; Bandura 1986), people are more likely to expend effort to achieve their goals, and to persist in the face of obstacles if they are high in 'self-efficacy'. The concept of self-efficacy corresponds to an individual's confidence in their ability to carry out specific tasks or behaviours. Bandura (1977) identified four main sources of self-efficacy:

Performance accomplishments/ mastery experience – experience of performing the target actions or behaviours successfully

Vicarious experience/ modelling – observing others performing the target actions or behaviours successfully

Verbal persuasion – receiving positive feedback on one's capabilities and achievements

Physiological and emotional states – able to manage feelings of stress, worry and anxiety

Self-efficacy is a central construct underlying patient self-management programmes, such as the Chronic Disease Self-Management Program (CDSMP) developed by Lorig and colleagues at Stanford University, California (https://www.cdc.gov/arthritis/interventions/programs/cdsmp.htm) and the X-PERT programme (to support diabetes self-management) developed by Deakin and colleagues in the UK (https://www.xperthealth.org.uk/)

The Common-Sense Model of Illness Representations

According to the Common-Sense Model (CSM; Leventhal et al, 1992), people form cognitive and emotional representations of illness which guide the methods used to cope. These include perceptions of the illness identity, cause, severity, timeline and perceived control, along with coherence (understanding of the illness) (Moss-Morris, et al., 2002). This model has been applied to understand individual variability in "adherence" to treatment regimens in people with LTCs. For example, research indicates that "non-adherence" is associated with perceptions of the illness as "mild" with low risk of complications, as well as lack of perceived effectiveness of treatments (Delamater et al., 2006).

Asking questions guided by the Brief Illness Perceptions Questionnaire (BIPQ; Broadbent et al, 2006) can be a useful first step for identifying beliefs contributing to psychological distress or limiting self-management in people with LTCs. Health professionals can be trained to use this approach to understand the individual's 'personal model' of their condition (what the illness and its consequences means to them) and deliver support that is tailored to the individual (Hamilton-West et al, 2013; 2014; 2018a).

Figure 1.3 Theoretical frameworks

challenge, as Health Psychologists may not have sufficient opportunity to apply or maintain these skills within their job role. For Health Psychologists employed in academic roles it is often difficult to develop opportunities to work directly with patients and service users (which is important for understanding the issues we set out to address and achieving real world impact) and such activities may even be viewed as a distraction from the 'proper work' of delivering lectures and publishing papers. Similarly, for Health Psychologists employed in clinical roles, activities such as conducting research, or attending conferences (which are important for maintaining disciplinary knowledge and keeping abreast of the evidence-base) may be considered a distraction from the 'proper work' of delivering patient care.

Both educational and healthcare organisations are subject to external targets and quality indicators (often linked to payment structures) which can act as disincentives to working more broadly as a scientist-practitioner. For example, it has been argued that the Research Excellence Framework serves to discourage applied research (Willetts, 2019) and direct scientific endeavour away from health conditions with low incidence, but high patient and societal impact (e.g. Conway, 2020). In the healthcare context, Gubb and Bevan (2009) argue that targets 'devalue the customer (patient) by focusing attention on an arbitrary number, devalue local leadership by relying on central control, and break systems into silos by focusing attention on parts rather than the whole' (p. 338). For people living with LTCs, this results in fragmented care provided by a complex array of services, with mental and physical healthcare needs addressed in a disconnected way (Naylor et al., 2016). Consequently, Health Psychologists involved in direct patient care often work within services and systems developed to treat *either* physical *or* mental health conditions, rather than services which are truly biopsychosocial. Such services are typically required to demonstrate value in relation to pre-determined outcomes (e.g. the number of patients achieving target blood glucose levels, or demonstrating clinically meaningful improvement in depression scores), rather than patient-determined outcomes (i.e. changes that are important to the individual; see Collins (2019). Wade and Halligan have further highlighted that:

> The boundaries between different organizations and budgets derive from the biomedical model and are increasingly based on the premise that healthcare is strictly limited to the diagnosis and treatment of disease. There is no acknowledgement that many real problems faced by patients and their families are multi-factorial and that a simple categorization (health/non-health) is inappropriate and impossible.
> (Wade & Halligan, 2017, pp. 1000–1001)

A further challenging facing Health Psychologists involved in direct patient care is the distinction between rhetoric (how concepts are discussed by researchers and policy makers) and reality (how these concepts are translated into interventions and services). For example, the concept of 'self-management' has been defined in various ways in the research literature and these definitions tend to raise more questions than they answer in terms of what self-management actually is (or what it is not). In policy papers, the concept of self-management is often used as a proxy for shifting responsibility for health improvement away from formal services and towards patients, making it their 'job' to self-manage and to do effectively, with minimal cost to the healthcare system (Hamilton-West, 2018a). Similarly, concepts which are commonly used within Health Psychology (such as self-efficacy) are not always well understood beyond the discipline. In order to communicate the relevance of Health Psychology research and theory to other healthcare professionals, we therefore have to find ways to bring these concepts to life (see Figure 1.4).

For the reasons discussed above, conducting applied work that is consistent with a biopsychosocial perspective and aligned with healthcare priorities (at individual/ organisational/ societal levels) can be extremely challenging. However, at the same time Health Psychologists are ideally placed to play a role in transforming healthcare and translating science into real world impact. In Figure 1.5, I suggest five key imperatives for Health Psychologists providing direct patient care, together with practical steps that can be taken to address challenges and harness opportunities.

Future directions for Health Psychology practice

> The need for change is clear. It is driven by the changing health and social care needs of the population, in which people have increasingly complex healthcare and lifestyle-related comorbidities which require long-term care. This requires a new approach to the delivery of care which is able to accommodate the growing demand for access and coordinate care around patients, families, carers and communities.
>
> (NHS Confederation, 2014)

The challenges facing health and social care are well recognised. For example, Public Health England (2017) reports that around two thirds of adults in England are overweight or obese, along with a third of 11–15-year-olds and a quarter of 2–10-year-olds. Obesity increases the risk of conditions such as cancer, heart disease, type 2 diabetes, depression and anxiety, with estimated annual costs to the NHS of £6.1 billion, costs to social care of £325 million and total costs to the economy of £27 billion (Public Health England, 2017). Population ageing is also associated with rising prevalence of LTCs, which affect around 80 per cent of those aged 65 and over (Department of Health, 2012). In addition, loneliness and social isolation are becoming increasingly prevalent and further impact health and wellbeing (Victor & Bowling, 2012). Reports highlight considerable overlap between mental and physical health –

In our work training health professionals to support self-management, we have found an origami task helpful for communicating the concept of self-efficacy.

Part 1: Minimal Instruction Conditions

As part of a workshop on psychological aspects of living with and managing long-term conditions, we ask participants to make an origami frog. Participants receive minimal instructions – they are instructed to work individually and not to help others.

After a few minutes, we ask them to stop and present their frogs to the group. Participants are asked to report what thoughts and feelings they experienced during the task and these are noted on a flip chart. Participants are also asked to rate their confidence in making origami frogs on a scale from 0–10.

Participants tend to report thoughts such as 'I can't do this', 'I give up', 'I'll just fudge it'. They report feeling frustrated, irritated, despondent, and typically report low confidence levels.

Part 2: Conditions Designed to Build Self-Efficacy

The task is then repeated under conditions designed to build self-efficacy. The facilitator demonstrates how to create the frog step-by-step (modelling), provides supportive feedback (verbal persuasion), encourages discussion of worries/concerns (physiological states) and continues until every person in the room as completed the task successfully (mastery experience).

Participants are then asked to present their new frogs; report thoughts and feelings experienced during the task and rate their current level of confidence in making origami frogs (0–10).

Participants typically report thoughts such as 'I've done it!', 'It actually jumps', as well as feeling supported, happy and confident in their ability to make origami frogs.

Part 3: Relating the Origami Task to Self-Management of LTCs

After completing the task under both sets of conditions, participants are invited to consider what thoughts and feelings a person living with a long-term condition might experience if they are expected to master complex self-management tasks without sufficient support (similar to the minimal instruction condition) and how these thoughts and feelings might impact behaviour. Participants often report that they would expect patients to experience thoughts and feelings like those noted on the flip chart at the end of Part 1 and that some patients might disengage from self-management attempts as a result.

Participants are then asked to reflect on what difference it made to complete the task under conditions designed to build self-efficacy and to consider how they could use this experience to inform the way they work with patients. Participants typically report that they gained greater insight into the reasons why patients might experience difficulties with self-management and why giving instructions is not enough (some have described the experience as a 'lightbulb moment'). Participants are also able to suggest ways in which they can adapt their work to incorporate the four pathways to self-efficacy.

See Hamilton-West (2018c) for further discussion and photos of origami frogs created by participants.

Figure 1.4 Communicating the concept of self-efficacy through origami

Imperative	Explanation	Suggestions/Practical Steps
1. Understand the system you work in	To apply your knowledge skills and competencies within the healthcare system, it is important to understand how this system works – e.g. how are NHS, Public Health and Social Care services organised, structured and funded, what activities are services contracted to provide, what types of activities are possible, or not, within each context, are there gaps in service provision resulting in unmet needs for particular groups?	The Kings Fund, Health Foundation and Nuffield Trust provide valuable resources for understanding health and social care.
2. Understand how your goals as a Health Psychologist fit with your organisation's objectives	Attending a conference, or engaging in research/innovation may be important for developing/maintaining your knowledge and skills, but what are the benefits for your organisation? You are more likely to achieve 'buy in' if you can make a clear case for support linked to the organisation's priorities and objectives. Be mindful that service managers face considerable pressures and there may not be funding/resources available.	Read your organisation's mission statement and strategy documents, discuss ideas with your manager. Offer to provide summaries/reports of events attended and share learning with colleagues across the organisation.
3. Build relationships within your organisation	In my experience, most people working in health services would prefer to provide care that is holistic, and patient-centred, rather than siloed and fragmented. If you are interested in finding ways to improve healthcare, you are likely to find others keen to work with you. Be mindful that you (and others) will need to obtain support from managers to take this work forward.	Talk to colleagues and take time to understand their experience and perspectives. Explain what health psychologists do. Provide evidence-based arguments to support your case – e.g. examples of related initiatives. Link activities to your organisation's objectives.

Imperative	Explanation	Suggestions/Practical Steps
4. Start small and build up	Small-scale audit/ evaluation projects can be valuable for sharing practice examples and building a research profile. Similarly, service innovation work can start with small scale pilot projects, using available funding and resources.	Look into potential external funding sources. Consider how small-scale research/ innovation work could be used to build a case for externally funded work. Contact your local NIHR Research Design Service for advice and support.
5. Disseminate to a range of audiences	To scale up research/innovation work and achieve impact it is important to disseminate outcomes in a range of formats, including publications, reports to funders/ commissioners, presentations to relevant organisations and groups (e.g. charities, patient support groups, professional networks) and online resources (e.g. videos, Plain English Summaries). Consider who your target audiences are and how best to reach them.	Work closely with stakeholders from the planning stage of a project through to dissemination. If you have a communications team within your organisation, speak to them for help and advice. Join a regional health psychology network.

Figure 1.5 Five key imperatives for Health Psychologists providing direct patient care

around 30 per cent of all people living with LTCs also have a mental health condition and this figure may be closer to 50 per cent for those with two or more LTCs (Naylor et al., 2012). People with LTCs find it harder to adhere to treatment regimens in the context of reduced psychological wellbeing and mental health comorbidities in people with LTCs have been linked to poorer clinical outcomes, reduced quality of life, increased costs to the health service and increased morbidity (Naylor et al., 2012; NHS Confederation, 2014). These challenges necessitate a shift away from care that is predominantly focused on treatment of single diseases, towards approaches that enable people to remain healthy, active and socially connected throughout their lives, including in the context of LTCs (e.g. Department of Health, 2012; NHS Confederation, 2014).

Health Psychologists have a vital role to play in this endeavour, by delivering evidence-based approaches to support health behaviour change, long-term conditions management and maintenance of psychosocial wellbeing. However, as noted above, providing patient care is only part of the Health Psychologist's role – it is essential that, as practitioners, we continue to adapt and refine our approaches according to the evolving evidence base ('the science'), the needs of each individual client ('the person') and the environment in which care is delivered ('the context') (see Figure 1.6). It is also essential that practice-based evidence is fed back to refine Health Psychology models and theory. Without this close interrelationship between theory and practice, we run the risk that researchers occupy the 'high ground' producing rigorous solutions to relatively unimportant problems, while frontline workers occupy the 'swampy lowlands' where important problems appear messy and incapable of technical solution (Schon, 1984). I would argue that bridging the gap between research and practice in Health Psychology is an important endeavour for all Health Psychologists, whether we identify as 'scientists', 'practitioners', or 'scientist-practitioners' – working together as a Health Psychology community strengthens both science and practice; it enables us to apply our collective disciplinary expertise (across a spectrum of individual areas of specialism) to find solutions to complex real world challenges.

Of course, in reality, we often encounter barriers that make it difficult to remain actively engaged in both research and practice. I have highlighted some of these in this chapter, along with suggested solutions/practical steps – these are not intended as a definitive list, but rather a starting point to encourage wider discussion and debate. I would encourage others to write about and present on the challenges they encounter as Practitioner Health Psychologists and to share examples of measures that have helped to overcome these.

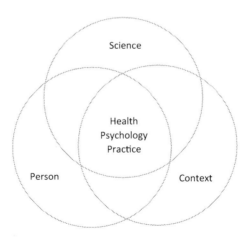

Figure 1.6 Health Psychology practice sits at the interface between science, person and context

I would like to end with an anecdote, which illustrates the need for further work to break-down barriers. In June 2020, the Royal College of General Practitioners (RCGP) held an online event entitled 'Covid-19: A lifestyle disease and the vital role GPs have in beating it'. Tweets to promote the event were met with a somewhat predictable degree of anger by GPs, other healthcare professionals, behavioural scientists, and members of the public who highlighted the offense caused by the term 'lifestyle disease'. RCGP subsequently issued an apology on Twitter for the inappropriate conference title and deleted tweets in which this appeared. In the discussion that followed, a few things became clear:

1 Although the terms 'lifestyle disease' and 'lifestyle factors' have been largely rejected within Health Psychology (due to the implication that disease is a 'lifestyle choice'), they are still widely used among GPs.
2 Many questioned whether these terms were inherently problematic (or only in the context of the conference title).
3 While Health Psychology research indicates that providing advice is rarely sufficient to change health behaviour, GPs are increasingly encouraged to 'prescribe lifestyle change' (e.g. offer advice on diet and physical activity).

How can it be, that after decades of research in Health Psychology and behavioural medicine (and more than 40 years after Engel's call for a biopsychosocial model of care), this disconnect still exists? A quick internet search of the conference title provides at least a partial answer to this question. The title drew criticism from many quarters, but a write-up in the BMJ only cites comments made by medics (Rimmer, 2020). Pulse magazine also reported on the controversy, but only GMC-registered doctors can access full content and post comments (Philpotts, 2020). Essentially, people are discussing the issue, but only within their own field. This is not a problem limited to medicine – as Health Psychologists we also hold our own conferences, publish in our own journals and so on. Of course, dissemination and discussion within the field is important, but it is not enough – if we want to achieve real world impact through our work, if we want to challenge the structures that leave 'no room ... for the social, psychological and behavioural dimensions of illness' (Engel, 1977, p. 130), if we want to deliver healthcare that is both patient-centred (appropriately tailored to the individual and context) and evidence-based (informed by relevant research and theory across the biomedical, behavioural and social sciences), we must challenge disciplinary and professional silos, engage in meaningful conversation with others beyond our field and reach out to those best placed to work with us improve outcomes for patients and the healthcare system.

References

Anderson, N. & Ozakinci, G. (2018). Effectiveness of psychological interventions to improve quality of life in people with long-term conditions: rapid systematic review of randomised controlled trials. *BMC Psychology*, 6, 11.

Bandura, A. (1977) Self-efficacy: toward a unifying theory of behavioural change. *Psychological Review*, 84, 191–215.

Bandura, A. (1986). *Social foundations of thought and action: A social cognitive theory*. Englewood Cliffs, NJ: Prentice-Hall.

Brassington, L., Ferreira, N., Yates, S., Fearn, J., Lanza, P., Kemp, K. & Gillanders, D. (2016). Better living with illness: A transdiagnostic acceptance and commitment therapy group intervention for chronic physical illness. *Journal of Contextual Behavioral Science*, 5, 208–214.

Broadbent E., Petrie K., Main J. & Weinman J. (2006) The Brief Illness Perceptions Questionnaire. *Journal of Psychosomatic Research* 60, 631–637.

Collins, B. (2019). *Payments and contracting for integrated care: The false promise of the self-improving health system*. London: The Kings Fund. Retrieved from www.kingsfund.org.uk/sites/default/files/2019-03/payments-and-contracting-for-integrated-care.pdf.

Conway, A. (2020). Health research funders should take more account of impact on patients. *Times Higher Education*, 9 January. Retrieved from www.timeshighereducation.com/opinion/health-research-funders-should-take-more-account-impact-patients.

Delamater, A. (2006) Improving patient adherence. *Clinical Diabetes*, 24, 71–77.

Department of Health (2012). *Long term conditions compendium of information*, 3rd edition. London: Department of Health. Retrieved from https://assets.publishing.service.gov.uk/government/uploads/system/uploads/attachment_data/file/216528/dh_134486.pdf.

Engel, G. (1977). The need for a new medical model: a challenge for biomedicine. *Science*, 196, 129–136.

Gubb, J. & Bevan, G. (2009). Have targets done more harm than good in the English NHS? *BMJ*, 338, a3130.

Hamilton-West, K. E., Rowe, J., Katona, C., King, A., Coulton, S., Milne, A., Alaszewski, A., Ellis, K. & Pinnock, H. (2013) A concordance therapy to help older people self-manage type 2 diabetes. *Diabetes and Primary Care*, 15, 240–248.

Hamilton-West, K. E., Smith, K., Vaughan, A., Kolubinski, D. & Kanellakis, P. (2014) Development of a primary care diabetes psychology service. *Diabetes and Primary Care*, 16, 129–136.

Hamilton-West, K. E. (2016) The role of a practitioner Health Psychologist in a primary care mental health service. *Health Psychology Update*, 25, 40–46.

Hamilton-West, K. E., Bates, A., Hotham, S. & Wilson, P. M. (2018) Development of a training programme for primary care mental health staff to support management of depression and anxiety in long-term conditions. *Primary Health Care Research & Development*, 20(e12), 1–7.

Hamilton-West, K. E. (2018a) How Origami Frogs Can Help Jump the Health Gap. *The Psychologist*, 10 July. Retrieved from https://thepsychologist.bps.org.uk/how-origami-frogs-can-help-jump-health-gap.

Hamilton-West, K. E. (2018b) Behavioural and social sciences should be part of medical education. *Times Higher Education*. Retrieved from www.timeshighereducation.com/blog/behavioural-and-social-sciences-should-be-part-medical-education.

Hinder, S. & Greenhalgh, T. (2012). 'This does my head in': Ethnographic study of self-management by people with diabetes. *BMC Health Services Research*, 12, 83.

HSPEC. (2013). Professional psychology in healthcare services: A blueprint for education and training. *American Psychologist*, 68, 411–426.

Hotham, S., Hamilton-West, K. E., Hutton, E., King, A. & Abbott, N. (2017) A study in to the effectiveness of a postural care training programme aimed at improving knowledge, understanding, and confidence in parents and school staff. *Child: Care, Health and Development*, 43(5), 743–751.

Katon, W. (2011). Epidemiology and treatment of depression in patients with chronic medical illness. *Dialogues in Clinical Neuroscience*, 13, 7–23.

Leventhal, H., Dienfenbach, M. L., & Leventhal E. A. (1992) Illness cognition: Using common sense to understand treatment adherence and affect cognition interactions. *Cognitive Therapy Research*, 16, 146–163.

Matarazzo, J. (1982). Behavioral health's challenge to academic, scientific and professional psychology. *American Psychologist*, 37, 1–14.

Moss-Morris, R., Weinman, J., Petrie, K. J., Horne, R., Cameron, L. D., & Buick, D. (2002) The revised illness perception questionnaire (IPQ-R). *Psychology and Health*, 17(1), 1–16.

Naylor, C., Parsonage, M., McDaid, D., Knapp, M., Fossey, M. & Galea, A. (2012) Long-term conditions and mental health: The cost of co-morbidities. Retrieved from www.kingsfund.org.uk/sites/default/files/field/field_publication_file/long-term-conditions-mental-healthcost-comorbidities-naylor-feb12.pdf.

Naylor, C., Das, P, Ross, S., Honeyman, R., Thompson, J. & Gilburt, H. (2016). *Bringing together physical and mental health: A new frontier for integrated care*. London: The King's Fund. Retrieved from www.kingsfund.org.uk/sites/default/files/field/field_publication_file/Bringing-together-Kings-Fund-March-2016_1.pdf.

NHS Confederation (2014). *Not more of the same: Ensuring we have the right workforce for future models of care*. London: NHS Confederation.

Philpotts, E. (2020). RCGP apologises after backlash over branding Covid-19 a 'lifestyle' disease. *Pulse*, 29 June. Retrieved from www.pulsetoday.co.uk/news/rcgp-apologises-after-backlash-over-branding-covid-19-a-lifestyle-disease/20041069.article.

Public Health England (2017). Health matters: Obesity and the food environment. Retrieved from www.gov.uk/government/publications/health-matters-obesity-and-the-food-environment/health-matters-obesity-and-the-food-environment-2.

Rimmer, A. (2020). Covid-19: RCGP apologises for covid-19 'lifestyle' event title. *BMJ*; 369.

Schon, D. (1984). *The reflective practitioner: How professionals think in action*. New York: Basic Books.

Victor, C. & Bowling, A. (2012) Longitudinal analysis of loneliness among older people in Great Britain. *The Journal of Psychology*, 146, 313–331.
Wade, D. & Halligan, P. (2017). The biopsychosocial model of illness: a model whose time has come. *Clinical Rehabilitation*, 31, 995–1004.
Willetts, D. (2019). *The road to 2.4 per cent: Transforming Britain's R&D performance*. London: The Policy Institute, Kings College London. Retrieved from www.kcl.ac.uk/policy-institute/assets/the-road-to-2.4-per-cent.pdf.

2 Health Psychology in an NHS pain management service

Laura Hissey

As a Health Psychologist working in pain services, I know that pain can have a profound impact on people living with it and those that support them. Every day, I see people of all ages from all backgrounds that are experiencing pain-related distress. It is a privilege for me to support them in their adjustment to living with pain and work alongside other professionals who support them to improve their quality of life.

The pain service accepts GP referrals for people with pain of six weeks or more, although symptoms of a much longer duration are common. I am part of a large multidisciplinary team (MDT) of pain specialists, including pain consultants, pain nurses, clinical specialist physiotherapists, acupuncturists and psychologists. It is our job to assess, treat and support people in developing self-help skills to control and relieve pain.

I provide specialist psychological assessment and intervention for people who are experiencing long-term pain conditions such as fibromyalgia, hypermobility and myofascial pain. I also work with people with more complex pain presentations such as phantom limb pain, Ehlers–Danlos syndrome and complex regional pain syndrome (CRPS).

One of the most exciting aspects of my role is that no two days are the same. My days are incredibly varied and often require different types of work. This can involve clinical work, teaching and training, attending meetings, service development and leadership responsibilities such as providing clinical supervision and managing psychology service provision.

Clinical work

I meet patients for the first time at an outpatient pain clinic where, as part of the MDT assessment, I undertake a detailed psychological assessment of their presenting pain. This includes understanding the background to the onset of pain and the impact that the pain is having on them physically, emotionally and psychologically.

At assessment, I am particularly interested in exploring what someone's perception of their pain is; their beliefs around what is causing it; whether they think it can be cured; and how they are currently managing it. The semi-structured assessment that I use to do this is largely based on the Common Sense Model of Illness Representation (Leventhal, 2003). This provides me with a useful framework to understand how someone's pain beliefs, treatment expectations and perceived impact of living with pain might be influencing their interpretation and response to it. Developing a comprehensive understanding of these factors helps me to identify potential areas for psychological intervention.

Each person has a unique story to share about the background to their pain. Some pain may have started following an event such as a car accident or major surgery; some patients may not know how or when their pain began, while others have very complex psychological backgrounds to their pain and have experienced torture, abuse or military combat. Inevitably for these patients, there is often a lot of trauma and mental health difficulties that co-exist with pain. It is very common for me to identify active trauma and untreated post-traumatic stress disorder in my psychological assessments. For this reason, I often work in collaboration with GPs, mental health teams and on occasion psychiatric liaison teams.

Undertaking psychological assessment in a pain population is complex and can be a challenge for several different reasons. Most commonly, there is a stigma for some patients around being asked to see a psychologist in relation to their pain. A lot of people are not expecting to be assessed by a psychologist as part of their pain clinic appointment. It is very often misinterpreted that being asked to do so is suggesting the pain is not real and is in fact imaginary. This can be further reinforced when my medical colleagues have been unable to give the patient a clinical diagnosis or explanation for their pain (which is very common in chronic pain) and investigations such as MRI scans have been shown to be normal. Many of the patients I see tell me that this causes them to feel not believed or listened to. This scenario is common and manifests itself in various different forms during my initial encounters with pain patients (e.g. anger, request for further medical opinion, disengagement with the pain service).

A very important part of my role at this initial consultation is therefore to validate pain and provide reassurance to the patient that I acknowledge that their pain is real. The majority of the people I work with have had their pain for a very long time and tried multiple failed medical treatments before seeing me. It's vital that I both acknowledge and empathise with each person's treatment history as it can be a significant influence on engagement with psychological intervention.

I spend a lot of time in my initial assessments explaining the role of psychology in pain management. To do this, I give a detailed scientific explanation of pain which highlights the role that mood (e.g. stress), thoughts (e.g. pain catastrophising) and behaviour (e.g. reduced physical activity) can have in aggravating the pain. This helps me to begin to engage people in a biopsycho-social understanding their pain and helps to normalise psychology input. I often use visual aids to present the patient's pain to them as a cycle (as opposed to a list of symptoms) based on what they have reported in assessment as to how it is impacting their life. For example, I explain how pain can lead to the patient becoming less active which results in a loss of fitness and muscle strength. This then creates a list of things which the patient cannot do and causes them stress, anxiety and frustration. Sleep problems, tiredness and fatigue can then occur. Negative thinking and fear about the future then cause low mood and depression; all of which reinforces the pain cycle and continues to maintain it.

Presenting someone's pain in this way helps me to emphasise to them that one small change can reverse the overall pain cycle. This tends to be a powerful exercise in empowering patients and shifting the patient's focus to areas of their life that they can change. I then introduce the idea of a self-care cycle which shows a range of strategies that can be used to break the viscous pain cycle and limit the impact of pain. This is often a pivotal moment in engagement with a self-management approach.

Managing patients' expectations at initial assessment can also be a challenge. It is not unusual for people to attend pain clinic with the assumption that their pain will be cured following their consultation with a pain specialist. This very often results in a (highly emotive) conversation around the nature of someone's pain. For example, that it is a long-term pain condition (identity), that is unlikely to resolve (timeline) and cannot be cured by medical intervention (curability) but can be managed with effective strategies. My main aim as a psychologist is to evolve understanding of pain from an acute medical curable problem to a long-term condition that requires proactive self-management.

Despite these challenges, the psychological assessment clinics are one of the most enjoyable parts of my role. I can see two patients in the same clinic with the exact same clinical presentation of pain on MRI scan. However, it can affect them in completely different ways. While one could report no impact of pain and be living a fulfilling life, the other might be experiencing overwhelming loss and report that living with pain has been life changing. Helping people to understand their pain and develop more helpful beliefs around it can significantly reduce the impact it has and improve quality of life. Being able to support patients to achieve this is an extremely rewarding part of my job.

Once I have completed a detailed psychological assessment, I produce a psychological formulation in collaboration with the patient which summarises their pain-related difficulties and helps make sense of them. I then attend a case conference with the rest of the multidisciplinary team to discuss treatment plans for each individual patient. In this clinical meeting, each specialist shares their clinical findings from their assessment; any concerns (e.g. co-morbidities, risk issues) and it is confirmed whether any further investigations (e.g. MRI scan, X-ray, blood tests) or medical treatment (e.g. injections) are needed. We all bring different perspectives and skills to help us plan how best to support our patients and their families. A management plan is then agreed by the whole team and forwarded to the patient and their GP.

Psychological intervention

I work therapeutically with patients in different ways depending on their needs. My clinical work includes one-to-one sessions, joint intervention working alongside other healthcare professionals and group work.

Within the psychology services that I am responsible for, I have implemented a stepped-care model of psychology intervention. This allows me to triage psychology referrals and allocate them to the appropriate 'level' of psychological intervention that is required. Intervention might range from a brief conversation with a psychologist in MDT clinic and signposting to online evidence-based resources, to intense psychological input for more complex needs. Complex psychological intervention would involve extended psychological assessment for several sessions, weekly 1:1 sessions and psychology leading and co-ordinating a care plan approach to treatment (with GP, mental health services and community services) around areas such as psychosocial barriers and risk management.

The patients I see for one-to-one psychology sessions present with a range of emotional and psychological difficulties related to their pain condition. This includes: struggling with the uncertainty of how their pain condition will progress or what treatment is available; feeling low in mood because they aren't able to manage activities that they used to; difficulty communicating pain to partners, family and employers; and difficulties adjusting to a change in lifestyle and identity as a result of having a long-term pain condition.

I use a range of psychological approaches in my work including cognitive behavioural therapy (CBT), Acceptance and Commitment Therapy (ACT), and mindfulness and motivational interviewing (MI). I always begin my one-to-one sessions by reviewing and discussing the formulation (from assessment clinic) with the patient and agreeing areas for us to work on. It is important that I outline a treatment plan along with aims and timescales. This helps to ensure that patients understand the aim of the intervention is not to cure their pain but for them to learn skills of how to manage it. I have to be very clear that the pain will still be there at the end of my intervention.

One of the most common needs that patients themselves identify to work on is stress. People with chronic pain often highlight the feeling of lack of control over their pain as one of the most stressful aspects of their condition. This can often manifest itself physically and lead to increased muscle tension and spasms which can then subsequently aggravate pain. Many of my one-to-one interventions therefore include relaxation training. This involves practising breathing techniques such as diaphragmatic breathing, progressive muscle relaxation, autogenic training and guided visual imagery to reduce muscle tension and promote the body's calming response. Alongside this I also teach general stress management techniques such as time management, problem-solving skills and assertive communication. Based on my experience, I find that relaxation is a strategy that most patients find very effective for managing pain. Increased muscle tension and postural changes are highly common among the pain patients that I see. I find that relaxation practice often results in positive physical changes quite quickly. This then helps patients feel more positive about managing their pain and is helpful for continued engagement in self-management.

I use a cognitive approach in intervention to challenge pain appraisals, beliefs, and expectations. It is very common for people to have negative thoughts about their pain. For many pain patients these negative thoughts become automatic and evolve into a habit of negative thinking. The most common thought patterns that I see clinically are pain catastrophising (*'it's hurting again; this pain will never get better'*); over-generalisation (*'I've had to stop exercising so I can't do anything anymore'*); and mind reading (*'they think I'm making the pain up'*). Once I have clarified any negative thought patterns, I work with the patient to learn how to identify these themselves using thought records. Once they are comfortable with this, we move on to practising to challenge them though enquiry and using evidence. I will often ask patients to keep a thought diary to help them develop this skill. We then look at constructing more realistic and helpful thoughts through looking for other points of view. For example, instead of *'I can't do anything anymore'*, it would be more helpful to think *'There are some things that I can still manage'*.

Again, this can be a very challenging part of my role. People can have very fixated beliefs about their pain. These can sometimes be unhelpful or even damaging. It is extremely common for people to have a misunderstanding of the identity, causality and curability of their pain (e.g. what is causing their pain and what can be done medically to help minimise it). For example, I have seen many patients who have been given a diagnosis of a 'slipped disc' and have misunderstood this medical term to mean that their spinal disc can freely slip and move in and out. This often causes significant fear and anxiety for people who believe that their disc can dislodge at any time and lead to excruciating pain. This then leads to fear-avoidance of doing activities. I have seen a large number of people who have unfortunately given up work, relationships and social life based on these simple misunderstandings of their condition.

Through my clinical experience, I've found that providing people with a biopsychosocial framework for understanding pain is very powerful in helping them construct alternative ways of thinking that are more helpful, realistic and adaptive. This is essential to help empower the patients and help them regain a sense of control back over their pain. It enables them to recognise that there are things they can do to help themselves and shifts their dependency away from medical treatment. This can help people rid themselves of their identity as a 'pain patient' and begin working towards an acceptance that, although their pain may not be cured, they can live a fulfilling life despite the pain.

Once we have developed a helpful understanding of pain, the focus is on acquisition of pain management skills. I teach patients how to pace their physical activity, set realistic goals, communicate their pain effectively to others and manage related thoughts and feelings.

Joint physiotherapy and psychology clinics

A lot of my clinical work involves delivering joint interventions with other pain specialists. Working jointly allows us to deliver more intense interventions for people with more complex needs.

I often work closely with specialist pain physiotherapists to help those patients whose pain is severely restricting their mobility and ability to function (e.g. to do activities of daily living such as wash and dress). This population of pain patients have often become reliant on care from others and have experienced a significant social impact of living with pain. For example, job loss, financial worries, loss of social relationships and hobbies.

Working jointly with the physiotherapy team ensures that we can deliver effective, targeted cognitive-behavioural pain management interventions. While psychology addresses the cognitive barriers to self-management, physiotherapy is able to work in parallel to target behavioural aspects; through offering advice and reassurance about movement and identifying practical ways that people can achieve their goals (e.g. providing equipment).

I also work jointly with consultants and pain nurses to support medical intervention for patients. Some people living with pain can become dependent on medication to manage their pain symptoms. Recent national data has reported an opiate crisis in the UK among people with persistent pain (Gov.uk, 2019) and the need to reduce prescribed opiates in pain has since been emphasised (Faculty of Pain Medicine, 2019). In response to this national directive, I have been supporting my medical colleagues by having a presence in their medication review clinics to help them in weaning patients off high doses of opiates. This has involved undertaking joint medical-psychology consultations to enhance patient engagement in self-management while developing a treatment strategy to reduce dependence on medication.

Group work

Group-based work forms a large part of my clinical diary. The psychology team co-deliver a 10-week pain management programme (PMP) based on British Pain Society guidelines (British Pain Society, 2013). As psychology service lead, I am responsible for the development, co-ordination, delivery and evaluation of the psychological components of these programmes.

A psychologist and physiotherapist jointly lead each three-hour session which provides educational talks, discussion and practical coaching in exercise, relaxation training, goal-setting and problem solving. The programmes take place in community settings such as church halls or local leisure centres and are run with groups of approximately 25 patients.

Discussion topics include how pain occurs, how pain affects the mind and body, how to manage stress, how to improve sleep, medication for pain and how to rely less on medication, how pain affects relationships and how to continue hobbies and work.

The PMPs are always a rewarding challenge. No two groups are ever the same. The biggest challenge is always engaging people in the self-management approach to pain which underpins the pain management programme. It is not uncommon for patients to be ambivalent about this approach when they initially start the programme.

Our discussion session on week one is always an interesting one; the session is focused on explaining the biopsychosocial nature of people's pain conditions and how self-management strategies can help. This can be met with a lot of resistance and scepticism from some participants. However, it is very important that we have these discussions early on to help align people's expectations as well as begin to challenge beliefs about pain and appropriate treatments.

The PMPs are a big-time commitment in terms of planning and co-ordinating. I have to triage all referrals to the programme to ensure that all patients attending are appropriate and that they are able to cope in a group environment. For example, if someone is experiencing severe social anxiety or anger management issues it is unlikely that a pain management programme would be a safe or beneficial environment for them. Similarly, if patients are still undergoing medical investigations or treatment for pain (e.g. scans or injections), it is unlikely that they will fully engage with the self-management approach which underpins the programme.

In order to ensure the psychology-led discussions are current and evidence based, I have to undertake regular reviews of new guidance and published research before planning the sessions. I also have to carefully consider the demographics of each pain management group and how the content might be received. For example, ensuring any examples relate to all cultural backgrounds and that all the topics are relevant (e.g. returning to work if the majority of the group are retired). Through experience, I have also learnt the importance of being aware of patients' reading and writing abilities as it is not uncommon for some people to be illiterate. I have also had patients attend with visual impairments. This presents a huge challenge when the delivery of the programme relies on reading handouts and engagement in writing tasks.

The delivery of effective group work is a very skilled aspect of the psychologist role. It requires an understanding of group processes and dynamics as well as skills in effective group facilitation such as active listening, social modelling, and summarising. Interpersonal skills including empathy, flexibility and the ability to confront are also vital to ensure that the sessions are contained and that participants feel emotionally safe. As a group facilitator I have to wear many different hats in helping groups make progress.

Teaching and training

Psychology-led teaching and training is an ongoing, key part of my role. I train and coach all staff in psychological concepts in several different ways which includes on-the-job training; large scale teaching programmes; clinical supervision; or group-based coaching.

Much of the 'on-the-job training' takes place in the multidisciplinary team case conference meetings after each assessment clinic. While giving feedback on the outcome of my psychological assessment, I often explain psychological concepts in depth to evidence base my clinical decision making. This also provides a good opportunity to educate the rest of the team to help deepen their psychological mindedness. For example, I have often educated my colleagues on theoretical models of Health Psychology such as the theory of planned behaviour to help the team understand how a patient's lack of perceived control over pain might influence the (passive) strategies which patients use to manage it; and therefore why my intervention would need to initially focus on enhancing perceived control and responsibility to enable a self-management approach.

In addition to continuous 'hands-on' training, I plan, deliver and evaluate formal psychological teaching programmes to the wider trust. These are usually in response to an identified educational need by a service or team.

Within the pain service, I have delivered a training programme to the pain nursing team on how to effectively introduce the concept of self-management to patients in medication review clinics. This was in response to feedback from nursing colleagues that they felt they were lacking the knowledge and skills to successfully introduce and engage patients in a self-management approach.

The training programme was delivered over 12 months as a series of four workshops quarterly which focused on introducing self-management concepts to patients, developing practical skills such as developing a collaborative relationship and teaching of basic self-management strategies such as breathing techniques. Post-training evaluation showed a significant increase in the nursing teams' confidence in their ability to engage patients in a self-management approach to managing pain.

On a wider trust level, I have enjoyed delivering large-scale training programmes in order to influence clinical protocol. Most recently, I worked in collaboration with our psychiatric liaison team to develop a suicide risk screening tool that could be used in outpatient pain clinics. This training programme was in response to an increased number of 'high psychological risk' patients presenting in outpatient assessment clinics. A screening tool and training programme was designed and developed to enable staff to be able to identify risk, extract key information and escalate it to the necessary services. Following the roll out of the training to the consultants, nurses and physiotherapy department the screening tool is now in use in all outpatient pain clinics. Clinicians have since reported that they find the screening tool and increased knowledge of risk management particularly useful in the absence of a psychologist.

My leadership role requires me to provide regular clinical supervision to the other psychologists working in the pain service. The coaching that I provide within supervision tends to be related to individual cases which each psychologist is working with and concerns therapeutic issues that have arisen during consultation. For example, this might involve help with developing a psychological formulation, providing support when working with a patient whose presenting pain is unfamiliar, exploring professional dilemmas or giving advice on trying new techniques.

I structure my supervision sessions so that they include some teaching on relevant Health Psychology theory. This has proved extremely useful given that I often supervise clinical psychologists who have not been exposed to such theoretical models as part of their training. I have found this a mutually beneficial process as it has also enabled me to learn a lot about the different therapeutic approaches that clinical psychologists are so highly skilled in.

I also provide weekly group-based supervision to the pain management programme team to help solve problems that may arise in group work and improve their confidence in the delivery of self-management support.

Leadership and service development

With ever-changing psychology service provision as well as changes in national guidance (National Institute of Health and Care Excellence, 2020) to how we support people with chronic pain, leadership and service development are integral parts of my role.

While the service I work for is generally well staffed psychologically, the demand for psychology appointments greatly outweighs the clinical capacity. This means that I have an ongoing responsibility to manage psychology provision across the service. This requires innovative leadership on issues such as managing waiting lists and developing waiting list initiatives (e.g. extra clinics); triaging referrals and liaising about the appropriateness of referrals (e.g. conversations with a GP if I think the patient would be better referred to mental health services); flagging shortfalls in psychological provision and prioritising need; adding concerns to the clinical risk register and notifying commissioners; and protecting professional boundaries around the psychologist role and caseloads. It is very common for me to have to manage expectations about what is realistic in terms of patient numbers for a Health Psychologist to see clinically. To do this effectively requires proactive leadership and good working relationships with colleagues.

I have an integral leadership role in staff and departmental meetings and I regularly make considerable contributions to case conference meetings regarding psychological care of patients in other services. For example, I am often asked to attend case conferences for patients who are being cared for by the acute pain team on a ward within the hospital but keep presenting at A&E after discharge requesting increased medication.

With regards to service development, I regularly review the psychology patient pathway within the service to ensure that it is effective, responsive and evidence-based. Within these reviews I consider how I can continually improve access to psychological services in pain and avoid long waiting times. Examples of this have included streamlining referral processes so that GPs can refer patients directly to me for psychology review as well as introducing telephone contacts to reduce wait time from referral to first contact. I also try to ensure that the psychological needs of different service user groups are recognised: for example, older people and ethnic minorities. This has been achieved through developing specific interventions such as pain management programmes for older adults and interpreted programmes for non-English speaking patients.

My other service development responsibilities tend to involve producing up-to-date service information for patients and potential referrers as well as helpful written patient information. I tend to signpost patients to online pain resources and communities so it is important that I am certain these resources are current.

Undertaking research is another aspect of my role. I thoroughly enjoy this aspect of psychology; however, I have found it very difficult to secure protected time to undertake comprehensive research when working in a clinical role. The type of research I have been involved in, to date, has tended to be service evaluation and audit, or projects in collaboration with local universities to inform aspects of service development. For example, a recent university collaboration about pain portraits demonstrated the clinical value in asking patients to draw their pain. This is now an additional dimension that we use in clinical assessment.

Summary

Working clinically as a Health Psychologist in a pain service is fascinating. The role is extremely diverse which makes it very fulfilling. Working as part of a large multi-professional team means that I am continually learning new skills and knowledge every day. The variety of my work pushes me to be creative and flexible in my approach and to draw on the different competencies that I learnt from my Health Psychology training. Through applied experience, clinical supervision and additional training, I have also been able to develop advanced clinical and interpersonal skills. This has enabled me to become a competent practitioner in working therapeutically with patients.

Moving forward, this is what I would like to see become more accessible for Health Psychologists; to be able to gain clinical experience and exposure to NHS practice and protocols while training. It is important that, as a profession, Health Psychology can add value in practice by applying our unique skill set to actually delivering clinical intervention, shaping NHS services and developing policy.

References

British Pain Society. (2013). *Guidelines for pain management programmes for adults.* London: British Pain Society.

Faculty of Pain Medicine. (2019). Opioids aware: A resource for patients and healthcare professionals to support prescribing of opioid medicines for pain. Retrieved from www.fpm.ac.uk/faculty-of-pain-medicine/opioids-aware (accessed 7 February 2021).

Gov.uk. (2019). Prescribed medicines: an evidence-based review. Retrieved from www.gov.uk/government/collections/prescribed-medicines-an-evidence-review (accessed 7 February 2021).

Leventhal, H., Brissette, I. & Leventhal, E. A. (2003). The Common-Sense Model of self-regulation of health and illness. In L. D. Cameron & H. Leventhal (eds), *The self-regulation of health and illness behaviour*, pp. 42–65. London: Routledge.

National Institute of Health and Care Excellence. (2020). Chronic pain in over 16's: assessment and management. Draft consultation.

3 The twists and turns into Health Psychology

Neesha Patel

This chapter provides an insight into my journey into Health Psychology in academia, and in the public and private health sectors. A single decision at the age of 18 changed the direction of my career, and little did I know what was ahead of me.

Introduction

'What do you want to be when you grow up?' This is a question a lot of children are asked at a young age by lots of different people. I was certainly asked this question but, even until the age of 18, I was never 100 per cent sure. A lot had happened during my early teenage years and at times it felt like I was just on the 'conveyor belt' of the education system, going from one period of education to the next.

Studying BSc psychology at university was never the plan until I got my A level psychology examination results, which clearly outshined the other vocational A levels which I studied for. It was at this point that I knew that I wanted to study psychology further, to better understand human behaviour and to help other people. I remember phoning UCAS and trying to get my first option of business studies changed to psychology. I travelled from London to Nottingham by train to the university's admissions office to complete some paperwork but, during my journey, I received a phone call from the admissions office to say that my request had been accepted. I was full of joy and knew this was my destiny calling – I still remember this day so vividly. I was also fortunate that my mother did not pressure me study a traditional vocational subject and had faith in my decision.

Two years into my degree I decided I wanted to do a placement year but, because this was a three-year degree with no placement, I had to initiate this myself and spent six months writing to several corporate business organisations that were offering work placements to business studies students – this felt ironic at the time. I applied for several human resources

DOI: 10.4324/9781003120469-4

(HR) positions as I felt this field aligned well with psychology, but I received several rejections with the main reason being that they were only looking for business studies students. Several applications and rejections later I finally got my break. I was offered an interview with Yell Ltd's HR department in Slough. I was so excited, but nervous about the interview, as I knew how much I wanted this opportunity, especially as it was not too far from home, and I could commute to and from work. The interview was a success and before I knew it, I had deferred my final year at university, moved back home, bought my first car, started a full-time job along with two other business studies students, and had the best year.

Upon commencing my final year, I felt recharged, grown up and, well, slightly more mature compared to when I had left and ready to face the challenge ahead; I was determined to work hard in my final year. I felt the 'new girl in town again' and went through the process of making new friends, as all my peers had now left and graduated. I also opted for the new module in Health Psychology led by the new lecturer Dr Richard Trigg. Little did I know that this module would be another turning point in my career. I really enjoyed learning about Health Psychology and the different areas of health that it can be applied to and the theories underpinning health behaviours. After despising physical education at school, I became quite a fitness fanatic and joined the gym after leaving school, practised yoga and developed a strong interest in healthy living. I think this is the reason I was so attracted to this module, as it connected with my values, and so decided to study it further by studying for an MSc in Health Psychology.

Once again, I embarked on the wonderful journey of applications, but this time also applied for stipends that were on offer to fund the Masters course, one of which was the one-year full-time Medical Research Council stipend at University College London. I was invited to interview for this stipend with Professor John Weinman and the late Professor Lynn Myers. I still remember this day, walking the vibrant streets around Goodge Street (central London) to find the building in which Professor Myers worked, for the interview; two professors whose work I read so much about in papers and textbooks. I was so nervous, and remember it being a tough interview (I was literally sweating by the time I finished), and the only question I can now remember being asked by Professor Weinman is 'where do you hope to be in five years' time?'. At the time I felt like I had regurgitated a sentence from their textbook, but they must have been impressed as I was offered the stipend and was so grateful. Little did I know how this experience was going to take my career into a direction that I had imagined. After accumulating a healthy amount of student loan for my undergraduate degree, I felt so lucky have this financial security to be able to solely focus on my studies without worry about finances, and to live the

London life. On reflection, I think that both professors must have believed in me more than I believed in myself at the time.

The experience of studying at one of the world's famous universities with world-renowned professors was an honour. The course was also affiliated with Kings College London and we had to attend a research methods lecture there every Tuesday with Dr Matthew Hankins. On some weeks it felt like going on a school trip travelling down together to the Kings campus after our morning lecture at UCL. I felt privileged to receive lectures from professors and lecturers who were experts in the different fields of Health Psychology for each of the modules covered in the master's course. However, the chronic conditions module is the one that I feared the most. My stomach used to turn during these lectures, especially the one on diabetes and chronic illnesses because of what I had witnessed in my childhood, and in my early teenage years. I wanted to refrain from studying the specifics of chronic conditions as I did not want to relive the memories associated with diabetes.

Diabetes is a word that entered my vocabulary at a very young age, just like the words, headache, cold and stomachache. From a young age I kept hearing this word because my father had type 1 diabetes mellitus (T1DM), but strangely it was my mother who used this word more often than my father. My mother took responsibility for his diet as she was the cook in the family and used to tell him when dinner was ready so that he could go and take his insulin injections before food. I remember when my father used to go to work in the mornings; I used to see an apple and banana on the dining room table, which my mother left out for him. I soon came to learn that diet was an important part of his diabetes management.

My father migrated to the UK from East Africa in 1972. Not long after coming to the UK, he was diagnosed with T1DM. At the age of 25, and as for most people diagnosed with T1DM, it was a life changing experience and one, which was, as far as I remember, managed with dignity. However, towards the latter years of his life, my father really suffered with his diabetes especially during the night. On several occasions my father used to have a hypoglycaemic episode and I remember jumping out of bed because I could hear him shouting for 'sugar' or talking deliriously about wanting some food. I remember frantically searching for Mars bars and running downstairs and fetching the tub of sugar from the cupboard and running back upstairs and my mother giving my father several spoons of sugar in water until he came out of the hypoglycaemia. It was very frightening to see my father in that state and not knowing what to do apart from reach for sugar and on a few occasions phone for an ambulance. Sugar seemed like the only cure at the time. The next day my father would tell us not mention his hypoglycaemia of the night before to the extended family members and he would often worry about the consequences of hypos causing some sort of brain damage, but I never knew the answers to his concerns.

In the early hours of one cold morning in December 1996 my father died of a major heart attack, the day after returning from a family trip to India with my mother and brother. My only understanding of his sudden death was because of his diabetes, and at the time it felt like diabetes took his life, because towards the later part of his life he was really battling with diabetes control. In my experience, in the last few years before my father passed away I could see sadness in his eyes; he became withdrawn and exhausted with life, and frustrated with his diabetes, especially his medication regime, and the frequent hypoglycaemic episodes he was having in the night and because of the lack of support from his GP who, ironically, also had diabetes. On reflection, I could see the areas of Health Psychology that were of relevance here – *clinical communication, illness beliefs, self-management* and *living with chronic conditions*, which fortunately are changing clinical practice across the NHS for patient benefit but deep down I felt frustrated and sad that it was too late for my father. From this point, I knew I had to make a choice: make peace with my grief and accept my feelings of discomfort and make the best I can of the opportunity given to me or walk away and do something different. I went with the first option.

Keeping up with the tradition of my undergraduate degree, I decided to seek voluntary work experience alongside my master's studies. I started work with Dr Hazel Gilbert at the Royal Free Hospital on a smoking cessation project funded by NoCLor. I assisted with the research-related tasks such as data collection, data entry, analysis and report writing. At the end of the project, we designed a poster to present our findings at the NoCLor conference. It was a good opportunity to use my research skills and gain experience of working on a funded project with a timeframe for completion and presentation.

No Health Psychology masters would be complete without information on doing Stage 2 training to become an independent Health Psychologist. Having been on both the receiving end and presenting on my experience, I know how valuable these sessions are in helping students decide whether they want to pursue with Stage 2 training.

Professor Weinman delivered our career in Health Psychology workshop and the burning question for most in the room was the possibility of getting a job in the NHS after Stage 2 qualification. At the time Health Psychology was celebrating 25 years of being in the field so it was slightly disheartening to hear about the lack of job opportunities in the NHS and the cost of the training to becoming a qualified Health Psychologist. For this reason, I decided to seek further work experience after completing my masters and graduating.

I spent a few months applying for applied psychologists' jobs but was unsuccessful and the feedback was usually that I had a lack of clinical work experience. It felt like all the education and work experience just was not enough and it felt quite frustrating and disheartening. I then decided to broaden the job search and look for jobs in health promotion, public health, and health behaviour change. I managed to secure a temporary position at Brent Council Children's and Families Department and assisted with administration duties before moving on to working in HR temporarily again for Police Information Technology Organisation in central London. I started to feel like my dream of pursuing a career as a Health Psychologist could not be further away; but I didn't give up hope. I tried to keep up with the job market and my hunt for a job in the health sector.

In 2007, I started working for Diabetes UK's head office in Camden (London) as an information assistant in the Healthcare Policy Team. Yes, Diabetes UK. I experienced the same emotions as I did during my masters about working in this field because of my emotional connection with this condition. I feared that I would not be able to fulfil my duties without detaching myself from the sad memories of what my father went through with his diabetes. Eventually I resulted to thinking that this job was part of my destiny or perhaps a signal from my father to work for an organisation, which he was not only a member of, but also an organisation from which he once gained support; support which he felt he did not get from the National Health Service. My main role was to assist with research into the health inequalities of diabetes services and engage with people with diabetes across the UK to improve access to services. I soon realised that something that once made me feel weak inside had now turned into my strength and determination to help improve self-management support, especially for people from the South Asian community. I also decided to find some voluntary work in the NHS to gain experience of working in a clinical setting with patients and other healthcare professionals. I started working for Michael Sorbell House Palliative Care Hospice at Mount Vernon Hospital, London. This was a unique experience in that patients who were terminally ill stayed here and my role was offer refreshments to them and their family who attended during visiting hours in the evening. It was strange as each week different patients would occupy the same bed or room and I knew the reason for this, but it was still sad and at times would remind me of my own grief and loss. However, the feeling of being able to help by making a hot drink and seeing the smiles on their faces was invaluable.

In 2008 came another turning point in my career. Diabetes UK hosted a workshop on motivational interviewing for diabetes healthcare professionals in Birmingham, and I went along to assist with the conference and this is where I first met Professor (then Dr) Christine Bundy, who was a senior lecturer at the University of Manchester (UoM) and a Health Psychologist. I was so impressed with how Dr Bundy had used motivational interviewing to train healthcare professionals to use it in clinical settings but also had first-hand experience of working with patients to support behaviour change using MI. I plucked up the courage to speak with her after the workshop to ask her about the prospects of doing Stage 2 training, and this is where she informed me about the PhD stipends that were coming up at the UoM and to consider applying and doing my Stage 2 training alongside PhD research training. I also started to explore the taught doctorate route at Staffordshire University and contacted Dr Mark Forshaw about the possibility of doing my Stage 2 training there while working at Diabetes UK. I knew there were going to be some exciting yet challenging times head. The feeling of something new was exhilarating to say the least.

Bumps along the way

To say that my journey has been a bumpy one is an understatement. I don't think any of us work in isolation from other life events that also need the same level of nurturing, if not more at times. I certainly don't think we are educated enough on coping with life events such as starting a family, being a parent and having a life outside of education and work. This was certainly the case for me when I got engaged and then had my big Indian wedding in 2008, and moved from London to Manchester and transferred to the Diabetes UK Warrington office. Soon enough I was back in the application seat, but this time to apply for PhD stipends. Yes, the time had come much to my family's concern about being a good Indian wife and studying at the same time. But as they say, love conquers all, and husbands need to be supportive, and I think my husband knew that I'd be incomplete without fulfilling my career goals and that certainly wasn't going to make me a happy wife.

It had been almost 5 years since I finished my MSc, gained some further work experience in a few different settings and some clinical work experience with 'real' patients. After my encounter with Dr Bundy at the Diabetes UK workshop and a few email exchanges, I felt inspired and motivated to apply for PhD stipends with the hope that my education and work experience to date would be sufficient to satisfy a panel of academics recruiting for a PhD student. But the pattern for success was no different this time. Application, interviews, and rejections. I mean I should have been used to this process by, now right. So, what didn't I have this time? Well, it seemed that stipends aligned to therapeutic models such as cognitive behavioural therapy warranted someone with experience of using the model with patients and this was one thing that I did not have. How naive did I feel? You know that feeling when you think you tick all the boxes and have a good chance of getting the job and 'boom!' the glass shatters? Well, this was me. I am sure I played some songs that resembled how I felt at the time. As always, I picked myself up and carried on. I kept in touch with Dr Bundy along the way who encouraged me to keep trying, which helped me to stay motivated. I replayed the clichés in my head to keep me on track: 'it wasn't meant to be', 'good things happen to those who least expect them'.

Finally, in summer 2009 I was offered a three-year, full-time PhD studentship at the UoM, Department of Primary Care, to embark on my PhD research proposal of improving self-management of diabetes in the Greater Manchester South Asian population supervised by a team of medical sociologists who had received funding from the Collaboration of Applied Health Research and Care, Long Term Conditions Theme. I was over the moon and filled with so much excitement of this new chapter that was yet to come.

I have always been a fan of Deepak Chopra. In September 2009, the quotes from his books certainly played true when I walked into my new PhD students' office. Little did I know that I would be sharing this office with Dr Chris Bundy who occupied a room in the PhD student office. My desk was outside her office. I knew it was fate. I mean what were the chances of this and what more could I ask for? In that moment, I knew that although Chris was not my official PhD Supervisor, there was no escaping a Stage 2 route. A bonus or torture alongside doing a full-time PhD, call it what you like, but it was not long until I was writing my plan of training for all my stage 2 competencies and submitting them to the BPS for approval.

The cliché 'be careful what you wish for' came to mind a few weeks after starting my PhD research. Being surrounded with Health Psychology lecturers and professors in higher education, I hadn't really given much thought to non-psychology academics and how they would view Health Psychology. On reflection, my experience of working with academics from multiple disciplines not only taught me how to grow thick skin and defend my work, opinions, ideas and goals for my research and Stage 2 training but to also learn that some things in life are like ice cream flavours – you have your favourites, the ones you learn to love, and ones that won't always be your first choice. You will also learn how to negotiate between the flavours and somehow still manage to enjoy and be grateful for the experience!

I must admit that I now appreciate the importance and usefulness of reflective practice. It is a core part of the Stage 2 training and, while doing PhD research, I think all aspects of education need to incorporate this to enable students to learn and grow from their experiences from a young age. Knowing that it is okay to make mistakes and to learn to do things differently next time may help to develop more secure, kind, compassionate and confident adults.

Towards the final months of the PhD write up, I had to make a conscious decision to park the Stage 2 write-up and the remaining competencies that I still needed to fulfil until I had submitted my thesis, as my PhD funding was coming to an end. Once my thesis was submitted, I applied for some internal department funding to support me with writing an NIHR RfPB grant application to extend an area of my PhD research. One area of my PhD research revealed some interesting information about fasting during the holy month of Ramadan and since my primary supervisor Professor Carolyn Chew-Graham was an Academic GP, she encouraged me to write up the findings into a qualitative paper for publication. The article was published in 2014, and lo and behold received extraordinary media attention both in the UK and across the globe. Before I knew it, I was being interviewed by *The Guardian* newspaper and other broadsheets like *The Independent*. I had never received any official media training but spent a bit of time with Chris Bundy who had experience of media work. I did several back-to-back radio interviews for a wide range of radio channels at Media City in Salford, Manchester including a live radio interview with BBC Asian Network.

Prior to the publication of this paper, I had submitted an abstract to the International Diabetes Federation Congress in Melbourne, which was accepted for oral presentation, and I also received a full bursary from the conference organisers to attend the conference. I was so excited to travel all expenses covered to sunny Australia. This exposure and experience felt surreal; I'd only ever heard about this happening with other people's research, but here I was in the limelight. I was nervous about working on platforms that I'd never been exposed to before but had to tell myself that I could do this. My subsequent PhD publications also received some similar media attention. This also led to some collaborative private work with pharmaceutical companies and education workshops for GPs in the northwest.

After the unsuccessful outcome of the RfPB application in 2013 (found out on the way to Melbourne on my stop over at Singapore Airport), I started working on a sleep and diabetes project in collaboration with the UoM and the Endocrinologist Dr Martin Rutter at the Manchester Diabetes Centre. This experience enabled me to fulfil my remaining Stage 2 competencies and once again work with patients in a clinical setting. I provided training to the nursing staff on using MI techniques as part of my training competency to enhance clinical communication and service user experience. I submitted my Stage 2 portfolio in summer 2014 and had my viva in November 2014, prior to going on my first maternity leave in summer 2015. However, a month before my maternity leave, I presented an education workshops on diabetes and Ramadan to some diabetes healthcare professionals in Preston. I met a diabetes consultant who showed a great interest in Health Psychology, and a few weeks later he set up a meeting with myself and the service manager of a newly formed Specialist Weight Management Service funded by local commissioning groups in Blackpool, Flyde and Wyre. I was then tasked with writing a job description for a Health Psychologist to join their multi-disciplinary team (MDT) to help them advertise and recruit for this post. I sought help and advice from SCCH Consulting on writing a JD for this role. Once the job had been approved and was advertised, I did not waste any time in applying. The interview process was not easy. I had to complete several tests online, attend a face-to-face, MDT panel interview while on maternity leave and a month later a second interview as there was a tie between myself and another applicant. Thankfully, I passed the interview and my dream had come true of working as a Health Psychologist in the NHS. 'YES, I have done it!', I thought to myself. I was on cloud nine for weeks after that.

On reflection, I do not think I had major expectations of the role, but did worry when I was asked to wear a uniform. Uniform? I thought, 'Psychologists don't wear uniforms, do they?' Staying with the metaphor of ice cream flavours, I soon came to realise that this analogy can be applied to a whole host of settings. I stood my ground and refused to wear a uniform, but this was a difficult battle to fight with a senior dietitian.

After being given a desk and chair on my first day, I spent several weeks designing the psychology pathway for this service and training the dietetic team on psychological aspects of obesity, as well as learning about severe-complex obesity myself. I used this experience to let other fellow Health Psychologists know about how they could seek similar opportunities and decided to submit an abstract which was accepted for oral presentation at the SCCH Conference in 2017. My confidence in working with patients on a one-to-one capacity grew by the day, and I was also fortunate to have excellent external clinical supervision with a senior clinical Health Psychologist, Dr Chris Gillespie, who practised at the Specialist Weight Management and Bariatric Services in Derbyshire. Joining the Manchester Health Psychology Skills Practice Group founded by Dr Eleanor Bull, Dr Anna Chisholm and Dr Jacqueline Levelle also provided me with the peer support and clinical skills training to enhance my job experience.

Before going on my second maternity leave in spring 2018 and returning to work in spring 2019, I reflected on my career to date and now of being a mother to two young children. No lecture while in education teaches us how to manage or have a career and be a parent. There is something to be said about having children and experiencing life changes when things at work remain the same or static. This is where I found clinical supervision to be most valuable as it made me reflect on how things had changed in my life; my identity and responsibilities, and how some of my frustrations with work situations were due to the position I found myself to be in my own life. After a month, I decided that something had to change. Commuting from Manchester to Blackpool, and having a young family, was not going to be feasible for long, and there I was back in the application seat on the hunt for a new job in the same field. I knew I was being ambitious. But as always, an opportunity did arise and this time it was with MoreLife Specialist Weight Management Service in Manchester, and I was offered the job as clinical lead and Health Psychologist. Even though I knew it was the right time to move, I still felt at crossroads with leaving the NHS and going to work for a NHS-funded organisation, as I knew this job was more about leadership and less frontline work with patients, which I loved so much. I took the plunge and started working for MoreLife in January 2020 and, before I knew it, COVID-19 had hit, and we were all in lockdown and working from home. New job, leadership responsibilities, home schooling, survival, Maslow's hierarchy of needs, you name it and I was doing it but with less red tape and more opportunities for innovation. It was like I'd been charged with creativity and a dose of personal growth at the same time. I grew to love podcasts, writing and recording my own podcasts on emotional eating, habits, and motivation with my fellow Health Psychology colleague Dr Sophie Edwards. The highlight of summer 2020 had to be my surprisingly unexpected TV appearance on the national BBC News as a Health Psychologist talking about the government's new obesity strategy. A proud yet nerve-racking moment, it felt like my PhD viva all over again!

Closing

As we near the end of this chapter, I would like to close on some final reflections and advice for future Health Psychologists, either those in practice and/or seeking clinical work.

I cannot tell you how valuable work experience is, whether you do a placement during your undergraduate, masters studies or post-graduation, being able to apply your interpersonal and professional skills with real people is where you really get to grow and learn. Seek a variety of settings to learn from. I have been fortunate with my work experiences to date, but I can tell you that it was not easy. It took a lot of time, commitment, self-motivation and self-drive to secure work placements and paid jobs to date. However, working with patients is where my passion lies as this is where I feel I can help change people's health and lives for the better. Having my Health Psychology 'toolbox' and everything that it has to offer, I feel empowered to help people to understand and reflect on their struggles and help them navigate through their difficulties to come to a place where they are happier and healthy individuals. I could not ask for more.

We are also very fortunate to be in discipline where we learn so much about communication and doctor-patient communication, which in my opinion is often the root cause of maladaptive behaviour in patients living with a chronic condition. Having good communication skills, both written and verbal, are an invaluable asset and will help you to succeed in anything that you do. How we communicate with people is so important in laying the foundations for that relationship whether it is personal or professional. Use the theories and information to your advantage; you are in the best field to learn about your own thoughts, feelings and behaviour. When learning a new therapeutic model, see how it fits in with your own life, self or situation that you may be struggling with. It makes it so much more authentic experience and easier to learn.

I have been very fortunate to have had amazing support from Health Psychology academics and peers who have helped and inspired me on this journey. Having a supportive network will help you to grow, face your fears, find inspiration, ideas, and opportunities. I think sometimes we try to do things in isolation either because we are too afraid to ask for help, share ideas with others or fear of rejection or being judged. We will all have at some point felt the dreaded imposter syndrome and read and attended lectures, workshops to overcome the feeling and thoughts about not being good enough or a bit of fraud. But I have come to learn to everyone sometime or another feels like this and it's okay. Trying to wear the 'expert hat' is exhausting and not sustainable in the long term.

My biggest advice is to do what you enjoy – it sounds like a cliché but it's so true. If you love what you do then you will be able to face any challenge that is presented along the way. Accept that there will be challenges and you will need to make short-term sacrifices to achieve your academic goals. Yes, you can be identified by your title, but the title does not define you, nor does it disclose the story behind your journey, success and heartaches. I would like to think after living and navigating our way through COVID-19 pandemic that we will have become more resilient humans.

ID
4 Delivering an NHS Health Psychology service for patients with eye cancer

Laura Hope-Stone

Introduction

This chapter is an account of working as a Health Psychologist (HP) in psycho-oncology at Liverpool Ocular Oncology Centre (LOOC) and as Health Psychology fellow in oncology at the University of Liverpool (UoL). It will demonstrate how a Health Psychology service can be integrated into an NHS ocular oncology service drawing on the biopsychosocial model, the mainstay of the discipline.

This chapter will describe my clinical work within one specialised service for patients with uveal melanoma (eye cancer) using examples of the theoretical frameworks that inform psychological assessment and intervention. It will also include the HP's role supporting patients making difficult medical decisions. The role has two overlapping reciprocal components, research, and clinical practice. As such, patient-reported outcomes (PROs) will be covered to illustrate this relationship. Lastly, the role of Health Psychologists in enhancing cancer care and adding value to clinical teams will be highlighted.

My route to becoming a Health Psychologist specialising in cancer care began when I was eight. My father, a consultant radiotherapist, took me to the radiotherapy department of the London Hospital Whitechapel. It was one of the most memorable experiences of my life. My recollection is not only the enormous imposing 'space-age' machines but also more tellingly seeing the children and adults with purple lines on their heads and bodies, delineating the radiotherapy fields used to treat their cancer. Six years later, after having read a biography of Marie Curie, my desire to follow a career in caring for people with cancer was confirmed. I subsequently went to qualify as a registered general nurse and specialised in oncology.

I was working as a senior clinical research nurse for the Cancer Research UK oncology centre at the Royal Free Hospital, London in the 1990s and had become increasingly interested in the interface between the

DOI: 10.4324/9781003120469-5

science, medicine and nursing and how patients were at the centre of this. Part of the role was to conduct quality of life research where I made my first foray into the world of psychological research.

While in post, I completed an undergraduate psychology degree at the University of Westminster, and following a career break undertook a MSc Health Psychology, Stage 1 Qualification in Health Psychology (QHP) at Liverpool John Moores University (LJMU). I proceeded with my Stage 2 training at the University of Liverpool and Liverpool Ocular Oncology Centre. As the post was set up for a trainee in 2010, I was able to gain four of the five QHP competencies: research; behavioural interventions; generic and professional; and consultancy. I gained the fifth, teaching and training, as a lecturer at LJMU. This was fortunate as the independent route to QHP with the British Psychological Society (BPS) often requires sourcing placements for each competency. However, the process was extremely demanding and, in addition to the academic challenges of doctoral level study, I was also responsible for delivering a Health Psychology service to patients in an internationally renowned specialist centre. I gained my QHP in 2013 and remain in post.

Background: the Liverpool Ocular Oncology Centre

Uveal melanoma is a rare cancer, and the most common intraocular tumour in adults which affects 2–8 individuals per million predominantly Caucasian people per year in Europe, and around 500 people in the UK (Virgili et al., 2007). It affects individuals with fair skin and hair who have difficulty tanning and with light blue, grey and green eyes. There are four tertiary centres in the UK and LOOC is the largest seeing over 50 per cent of new cases. Most patients are referred to LOOC by their local ophthalmologist having experienced visual disturbances. However, around 30 per cent are asymptomatic and are referred following a routine optician's appointment (Damato 2001, 2010). Once referred, they are usually seen within 1–4 weeks. LOOC holds a new patient one-stop clinic every Monday. Before the appointment, patients are sent a guide to eye tumours and its treatment. As patients come from all over the UK most would have spent the night before their appointment in a hotel. They are advised their clinic visit could last up to 6 hours and they should be prepared for a 5–7-day stay in hospital should treatment be scheduled for the following day.

On arrival at the one-stop clinic patients progress through a series of steps with specialist ocular oncology nurses, photographers and surgeons. They undergo tests including visual acuity and photography. A clinical history is taken, and examination follows. Lastly, patients are seen by the consultant who will show them the photograph of their eye and lesion, and based on all the information gathered tell them the likely diagnosis. Some will be told it is a 'naevus', a benign lesion, others will be told that it is an 'indeterminate' lesion which can be monitored, biopsied (to establish diagnosis) or treated. Another group will be given a clinical diagnosis of a uveal melanoma (UM) and offered treatment based on the tumour characteristics. The aim is to conserve the eye with useful vision and around 70 per cent will be offered radiotherapy. However, around a third of patients will need an enucleation (eye removal) (Damato & Heimann, 2013). While the primary tumour can be successfully treated, around 40–50 per cent of patients will develop metastatic disease, usually in the liver and treatments rarely prolong life. (Kujala et al., 2003; Singh et al., 2011). Many patients therefore are offered a prognostic biopsy to establish the risk of developing liver metastases over the next 10 years (Damato et al., 2011)

Following diagnosis, patients will spend time with ocular clinical nurse specialist (CNS) who will go through in detail the treatment and potential side effects. They provide immediate emotional support to the patient and family.

The impact of the speed and the intensity of this one-stop clinic cannot be underestimated. Patients commonly describe it is as a 'whirlwind', a 'roller coaster' and feel 'shell-shocked'. They have often come from a high street optician to a cancer diagnosis in a short time. Patients, as well as coping with an often unexpected cancer diagnosis, may also have to adjust to changes in vision and/or appearance. There is also the threat of developing metastatic disease with limited therapeutic options available.

The role of the Health Psychologist at Liverpool Ocular Oncology Centre

In 2004 the post was established at Liverpool Ocular Oncology Centre (LOOC) at St Paul's eye unit Liverpool University Hospitals' Foundation trust (LUHFT) in collaboration with the Department of Clinical Psychology at UoL. This was to ensure the Health Psychology clinical service was firmly rooted in a robust research environment and, to ensure the research programme was relevant to the clinical needs of patients and reflected the values of the broader ocular oncology service. The research and clinical components of the post are equally split.

The Health Psychologist (HP) was employed to: offer psychological assessment and early intervention to every patient diagnosed with uveal melanoma as well as conduct research, service development and provide consultancy to staff. By making it accessible to all patients, the aim was to present a 'routine' service offered to everyone newly diagnosed with an ocular tumour and seen as part of 'normal' care. It was a deliberate departure from the traditional clinician-referral route in the mental health model of providing one-to-one therapy to a few people. This was integral to the identity of the role making it distinct from mental health services and clinical psychology (Cook et al., 2008).

As the service evolved, other routes to access to the Health Psychology Service (HPS) have been established. Patients can self-refer or be referred by clinicians at any time while they remain under LOOC's care. Because many patients live far away, psychological intervention is mostly by telephone (Watson et al., 2013; Watson et al., 2017). Therefore, it is accessible to all patients regardless of geographical location.

The evidence base and theoretical framework informing the everyday 'routine' clinical work: an approach to assessment, formulation and intervention

Following diagnosis, all patients are given an information leaflet about the Health Psychology Service (HPS). Most patients are admitted for in-patient treatment and I see them following surgery and carry out a Health Psychology assessment if the patient agrees. I contact the remaining patients who do not require hospital admission 1–2 weeks following diagnosis to offer an assessment appointment.

Guided by Peter Salmon, and my predecessor Sharon Cook, two key models inform the assessment: Shontz's stage theory (Shontz, 1975) and Lazarus and Folkman's (1984) cognitive-appraisal model of stress and coping.

As a trainee psychologist, while considerable nursing experience and feeling very much 'at home' in the clinical setting, I felt Shontz's model made sense of the initial shock of the diagnosis. The model considers that, when faced with a diagnosis of cancer, individuals adapt in three stages. The first stage is of 'shock' when patients can seem distant and disoriented followed by a period of overwhelming emotion: the 'encounter' stage. A third phase is when patients protect themselves from the intensity of the emotion: the 'retreat stage'. Individuals do not necessarily fit neatly into stages and patients pass naturally from one to another many times. I need to discern what stage they are in, normalise and validate that stage. While it helps frame the person's experience at any given time it does not inform whether they will need psychological help. To gain a better understanding of how patients will respond and cope with the diagnosis and a potentially life-threatening disease, a more functional model is needed to inform the formulation and intervention, if needed. This is where the stress and coping model comes to the fore.

For every newly diagnosed patient, a crucial component to the assessment is recognising whether patients have coping resources that allow them to adjust and recover over time, and it is imperative not to undermine this natural process. My assessment therefore needs to determine if patients can draw on their own psychological personal and social resources to enable them to adjust without help. The model provides a framework to formulate the key elements as to how patients are likely to cope in the future. The assessment considers that distress may be a part of the adjustment process; it is not uncommon and can be a normal, adaptive response that resolves without intervention (Brennan, 2004; Salmon, 2000).

As a Health Psychologist a central tenet is the ability to predict, ideally prevent and if needed, treat psychological morbidity or 'distress'. Distress incorporates a range of emotional and cognitive responses defined as any negative mood state, including anxiety, depression, trauma symptoms and global distress (Fisher et al., 2020).

Predicting who is vulnerable to future distress and whether patients have the resources to cope is a fundamental component that underpins my decision to offer 'early' intervention following assessment. I am to some extent guided by the literature in cancer generally about potential risk factors for poor adjustment and persistent distress such as poor social support (Nordin et al., 2001), anxiety and depression around the time of diagnosis, personality traits predisposing patients to anxiety, and history of premorbid psychological problems (Cook et al., 2018). In uveal melanoma specifically, younger age and female gender, treatment related symptoms and worry about recurrence are also implicated (Hope-Stone et al., 2016; Brown et al., 2020). However, while this evidence informs my work it is too limited to provide a precise predictive algorithm for use in clinical practice. Therefore, my clinical judgment as to how patients may cope in the future needs to reflect the context and characteristics of individual patients (Hope-Stone et al., 2019a).

This process of assessment and formulation is demanding when time with each patient is often limited due to radiation safety and the ward environment not always conducive to private conversations. Taking a glimpse of someone's life when they are potentially at their most vulnerable is humbling. Every ounce of tact and sensitivity is needed so as not to undermine or interfere with normal ways of coping or, intrude unduly into their lives uninvited.

Assessment and intervention: the cognitive-appraisal model of stress and coping

To illustrate the relevance of the model in clinical practice I have used a case formulation (Figure 4.1) for a newly diagnosed patient. Two processes are central to the model: appraisal (primary and secondary) and coping. Stress arises when individuals notice a potential change in their

An NHS service for eye cancer patients 47

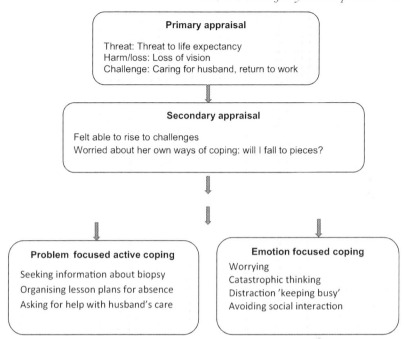

Figure 4.1 Case study: assessment and case formulation
Primary appraisal: stressors appraised as severe threats and actual harms and losses associated with potential threat to her life expectancy and loss of vision. Challenge appraisals were associated with the need to work and care for her husband in the long term. Secondary appraisal: Julie felt she could rise to the challenge of the practical implications of her diagnosis and treatment but questioned her ability to cope with the threat of cancer spread. These appraisals led to a blend of problem- and emotion-focused coping.

relationship with their environment. Primary appraisal is an evaluation of the personal significance of this change and determines whether a situation is viewed as a threat, whether there is a potential for actual harm or loss, or whether it is seen as a challenge to be overcome. Secondary appraisal is an evaluation of an individual's coping options; determined by whether individuals feel they can control and change the situation and rise to the associated challenges. According to Folkman and Greer (2000), individuals who feel they can do this use active coping approaches such as information seeking. Those who feel they lack control over their circumstances tend to engage in emotion-focused coping such as support seeking and avoidance. The appraisal process also engenders emotions; a loss appraisal is associated with anger and sadness, and threat appraisal with anxiety and fear.

The intensity of these emotions will also influence how individuals cope (Lazarus & Folkman 1984). Furthermore, appraisal and coping are influenced by internal and external factors such as prior experiences, beliefs and personal and social resources. As part of the assessment, I use the Hospital Anxiety and Depression Scale (HADS) (Zigmond & Snaith, 1983), used widely to screen cancer populations (Vodermeier & Millman, 2011). I interpret the HADS score considering contextual information related to but not confined to their cancer diagnosis (Hope-Stone et al., 2019a).

Julie is a 56-year-old Mathematics teacher diagnosed with a uveal melanoma following a routine eye test and was treated with plaque radiotherapy which required admission to hospital. She had not decided whether she would have a prognostic biopsy. Her husband is unable to work due to spinal injury and Julie is the 'breadwinner'. Julie describes herself as a 'worrier' but does not like to burden those closest to her with her concerns.

Julie appeared very tense post-operatively. Her main concerns were future loss of vision and the potential for cancer spread and the implications for her husband. During the assessment, it became apparent that Julie had been using a problem focused approach to coping which helped her feel in 'control' and included developing lesson plans for her pupils, online shopping and organising care for her husband. However, she was alarmed by her emotional response. She felt she might 'go to pieces' and 'buckle' and reported a constant cycle of catastrophic thoughts. She was reluctant to express how she was feeling to her family, as she did not want to be seen as 'not coping' and cause them more distress. Julie explained that her sister had been trying to 'jolly her along' insisting that she 'think positively'. This did not come naturally to Julie thus compounding her feelings of inadequacy and she felt she was 'failing'. She had not told close friends or colleagues as she was worried about 'breaking down'. Her scores on the Hospital Anxiety & Depression Scale (HADS) (Zigmond & Snaith, 1983) were above the clinically relevant threshold for anxiety and within normal range for depression (Vodermeier & Millman, 2011). Following the assessment, we agreed further intervention was needed to help Julie cope and adjust to her diagnosis and treatment.

Intervention

An essential element of the subsequent intervention of four further sessions over a period of eight weeks aimed to provide a supportive context for emotional disclosure, to express freely her concerns about her uncertain future, facilitate adjustment by normalising and validating her emotional responses. Additionally, we used the time for Julie to reflect on her coping, and what she found helpful, and introduced ways of managing her negative catastrophic thoughts with strategies such as worry postponement and 'noticing' thoughts rather than engaging with them. Over time, she felt more able to cope with her emotional response and recognised that these responses were integral to her adjustment process.

Since its inception, the HP role has evolved considerably. The focus originally was seeing all new patients. However, this access was extended to any patient with an ocular tumour under the care of LOOC. Patients can self-refer or be referred by specialist nurses and clinicians. Purposefully, this process is kept simple to reduce barriers and facilitate accessibility, and thus ensure I can respond flexibly to patients' needs as they arise. This could be in the early stages following diagnosis, but many referrals come later, initiated by patients or clinicians. Referrals often come from people who have become 'stuck' and unable to move forward with their lives. Patients must adapt to many changes in their lives including visual impairment, ocular symptoms, changes in appearance as well emotional changes arising from worry about local recurrence and metastatic disease. For many patients, the time after the initial period when treatment has finished can be as difficult as it was in the early stages. People often have more time to think about what they have been through and can experience strong emotions. Patients need to learn to live alongside these difficulties and worries. This is where I find it useful to draw upon Brennan's (2001) social-cognitive transition (SCT) model of adjustment to help patients conceptualise and understand their reactions as they strive to 'get back to normal'.

Brennan's social cognitive transition model of adjustment

The SCT model draws on ideas and concepts from existing models of adjustment, coping theory, post-traumatic stress, social cognitive theories and cognitive theories of emotion. It has been developed to knit together a model of adjustment, with cancer as the source of the traumatic event. Rather than an endpoint, Brennan (2001) considers adjustment as a process that includes behavioural and cognitive adaptations, taking into account the social context. Humans learn from experience and over time develop schematic representations of the physical and social world or 'core assumptions' that form an individual's assumptive world.

During their life span, individuals acquire a complex set of mental maps or schema which are revised constantly. These enable people to plan, predict and maintain reasonably constant experiences of the world, their beliefs and how they see their future. These assumptions are reinforced when expectations are met. Some people have flexible assumptive worlds

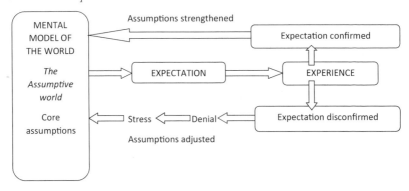

Figure 4.2 Social-cognitive transition model of adjustment
Source: Brennan (2001)

and can more readily accommodate novel information; others are more rigid, and many factors are instrumental in building a 'complex matrix of assumptions' (Brennan, 2001, p. 8). A cancer diagnosis, like any other traumatic or shocking event, destabilises and interrupts these assumptions and the schema cannot be relied upon. Individuals have a huge range of responses to traumatic events which are associated with three key factors. First, people hold differing views of themselves, others and the world. Second, life events are experienced within a variety of social contexts (e. g. gender, race and healthcare provision). Third, individuals have diverse styles of responding to information that threatens their assumptive world.

According to the SCT model, adjusting to these alterations in assumptions causes stress and arousal, involving a great deal of cognitive processing and emotional distress. The way in which people deal with this onslaught is to filter the amount of disturbing information. It has been theorised that adapting to traumatic events involves two processes: avoidance and intrusive thoughts. As individuals vacillate between the two, traumatic information can be tempered and gradually assimilated into their core beliefs (Jim & Jacobsen, 2008). Similarly, denial, in the SCT model, acts as a defence mechanism. It is seen as an adaptive response and usually a short-term means of aiding individuals to integrate and process the shocking events to become part of their assumptive world, albeit a changed one.

It is important to highlight, and evident in my work, that a cancer diagnosis and adjustment process can lead to positive changes or post-traumatic growth. For many, a diagnosis of eye cancer can lead to a change in attitude about what is important as priorities in life shift.

Once again communicating the key elements of the model to patients requires skill and sensitivity tailored to patients' individual adjustment processes so as not to pathologise their responses or undermine normal adjustment.

Decision making: a role for Health Psychology

When patients are diagnosed with uveal melanoma, they sometimes need to make difficult and potentially life changing decisions. It could be treatment related or more commonly, it is whether to undergo a prognostic test to determine life expectancy. Many people make decisions easily, for others it is hard and patients are referred to me if needed.

Decision making and prognostication in uveal melanoma: interface between research and clinical practice

While the primary tumour can be successfully treated, the unfortunate reality is that around 40–50 per cent of patients will die of metastatic disease. It usually spreads to the liver first and, currently there are no proven efficacious treatments.

Patients are offered a prognostic test, which involves a tumour biopsy to estimate with a high degree of accuracy their life expectancy over 10 years. Patients need to decide whether they would like one. The treatment for the primary tumour has no bearing on the results. For example, patients choosing between radiotherapy and enucleation are told regardless of treatment this will not affect their long-term survival. So, how do patients decide and what is the Health Psychologist role in supporting patients to make the 'best' and the most 'reasonable' decision they can? Early on my role, it was apparent that patients did not fully understand the decision they were being asked to make. This was of great concern as I considered the moral and ethical implications. Furthermore, work done by my predecessor had highlighted these dilemmas.

Models such as shared decision making (SDM) emphasise the importance of patient participation in the decision-making process (Elwyn & Miron-Shatz, 2010). The SDM is considered a cornerstone of upholding the principles of autonomy and informed consent. It evolved as a response to paternalism to involve patients in decision-making tasks especially when potential benefits are uncertain or unclear (Elwyn & Miron-Shatz, 2010). This brought into sharp focus the considerable uncertainty about many healthcare interventions.

However, SDM assumes that a decision is negotiated equally. The professional is the 'expert' who provides information; the patient 'non-expert' takes account of the information accurately weighs up the likely risks and benefits and subsequently comes to a decision. Patients are thus able to make an 'informed' decision and can provide informed consent and have, above all, exercised autonomy. However, autonomy is not without its difficulties. First, providing information is often conflated with informed consent and may give the impression that the patient has more control (Doherty et al., 2017). Second, patients find it uncomfortable that the responsibility for making treatment decisions is theirs, based on information they may not fully understand (Sinding et al., 2010) and often do not want to make decisions themselves (Cook et al., 2011; Doherty et al., 2017). Third, SDM assumes an equal partnership but clinical relationships are frequently asymmetric (Pilnick & Dingwall, 2011) and often reflect social hierarchies.

The assumption that decision-making is a logical, practical process whereby rational decisions are made has been challenged. Evidence is emerging that individuals use informal heuristics (i.e. mental short cuts that help people respond to complex information; Brown & Salmon, 2019). For example, in making judgments about risk. Examples of these are the 'affect' heuristic whereby people infer risk based on their emotional responses (e.g. fear, worry), with stronger emotions associated with enhanced risk, or the 'availability' heuristic when people judge their risk based on information recalled from memory such as a family history of cancer or a report in the media and thus the judgement is heavily context dependent (Peters et al., 2006). Arguably, therefore the use of heuristics is irrational as by over-simplifying complex information patient autonomy could be compromised (Brown & Salmon, 2019; Swindell et al., 2010; Schwab, 2006).

Against this background of conflicting evidence, I need to support patients making difficult decisions about treatment and/or prognostication. I am often asked by patients to provide an account of how it affects people given differing prognoses. I can cite population-level findings but while there is some evidence that levels of depression, anxiety and worry about recurrence are higher in patients with a poor prognosis, a larger study is needed (Brown et al., 2020; Hope-Stone et al., 2016).

My role, however, is supporting individuals. When a patient is referred for 'help with decision making about the biopsy' a typical session would involve assessing: their understanding of the decision they need to make; how they may normally make decisions; what and who influences their decisions. It entails 'affective forecasting' (i.e. exploring people's expectations of how different outcomes will affect them; Hoerger et al., 2016). For example, anticipating regret for not undergoing the biopsy or questioning their own ability to cope with a poor prognosis. Affective forecasting, though, is not without its pitfalls. Arguably, it provides a 'snapshot' of an imagined future though a small window based on their emotional state at the time of the assessment whereupon they may over-estimate their future distress or conversely, in relation to coping, underestimate their own resilience.

Furthermore, patients' subjective interpretation of their own risk of developing metastatic disease may not match their objective risk and thus responses to prognostic results are hard to predict (Hope-Stone et al., 2015b). I therefore take the 'forecast' into consideration accounting for an individual's wider context. Often, patients want to feel validated that they have had time to think through the implications of the decision.

An integral part of my HP remit is to develop accessible information for patients. Decision aids have an important role; and it was evident that a clear, coherent information resource for patients offered the prognostic test was needed. This is a complex test and it was apparent that many patients had not fully understood the test and its potential outcomes. Additionally, patients sought information online and were making decisions often based on inaccurate, out-of-date information. With that in mind and to ensure consistency, in collaboration with the wider LOOC team we developed a patients' guide to prognostication. This was a challenge; I needed to simplify complex biomedical information without presenting it as a 'simple' decision. To bring it to life with the hope it would resonate with individual patients we presented vignettes of patients with different personalities, contexts, values, preferences and ways of coping. This guide will be revised as the findings emerge from a qualitative study we undertook to examine in detail how and why patients decide to accept or decline the prognostic test. This illustrates again the link between the clinical and research components of my work. Crucially, patient information alone is not a substitute for support. All patients are offered an appointment with me and intervention, if appropriate, is informed by the wider literature as well as our own research specifically into decision making in prognostication.

Patient-reported outcomes

I am in a privileged position to be part of a group at UoL specialising in psycho-oncology and have access to expert academic support with invested colleagues and supervisors. A substantial part of my research role is to manage the PRO studies and I was fortunate to join LOOC at the same time as an extremely efficient research assistant (NL). Ocular oncology has its own database storing clinical and biomedical information with just one data manager (GC). Additionally, it holds the PRO data from paper questionnaires specifically measuring distress, general and eye-related quality of life. NL and I were charged with checking the fidelity of the data to ensure we had a dependable accurate dataset to conduct analysis.

We have strived to ensure the research questions we pose are relevant to our clinical population. For example, the lead clinician asked us to examine PROs comparing enucleation versus proton beam radiotherapy (Hope-Stone et al., 2018b) and the effects of phantom eye syndrome on enucleated patients (Hope-Stone et al., 2015b).

With confidence, the clinicians and I can talk to patients about findings of the PRO studies. When patients ask, 'How do other people feel after diagnosis and treatment?', on a population level we can say that by six months after finishing treatment, most patients have at least as good a quality of life as people without this condition; the type of treatment does not generally influence mood (Hope-Stone et al., 2016); that prognostic information affects people in different ways (Hope-Stone et al., 2015b; Brown et al., 2020). We know that people who have more eye-and vision-related difficulties are more likely to worry about the cancer coming back (Brown et al., 2018). Taken together our studies have enabled us to inform patients of the likely clinical and psychological outcomes patients can expect.

Our PROs research continues but the focus of our attention has shifted to explore predictors of distress and we are investigating potentially modifiable psychological processes that underpin persistent distress. Together with clinical psychology colleagues, we are examining the role of metacognitions and illness perceptions and how they interact with eye-related QoL, clinical and prognostic factors in persistent distress. This will guide development of psychological interventions for patients. For example, therapeutic approaches targeting metacognitive processes such as metacognitive therapy (MCT) (Fisher & Wells 2009; Wells 2011).

Multi-disciplinary team working, supervision and reflections

One of the most rewarding aspects of my work is being fully integrated into the multi-disciplinary team. My role is seen as part of normal care, and I can be responsive and available to patients and staff as needed. This close collaboration is helpful as it is common that patient will ask about clinical issues if they are worried about them. I can answer some of these queries and can easily refer onto the specialist nurses.

I am also part of the wider clinical health psychology (CHP) team at LUHFT. This service originated from a cancer psychology service set up in 2009 and now comprises clinical psychologists, assistants, trainees, a counselling psychologist and two Health Psychologists working across a wide range of physical health conditions. The wider team affords the opportunity of sharing reflections, knowledge and insights with other psychologists.

The nature of my role brings a degree of ambiguity regarding autonomy. I need to balance my autonomy as the sole psychological practitioner in ocular oncology, while working as part of the CHP team. I am in a privileged position as to how I manage my clinical contact with patients. I have the freedom to respond flexibly to the changing needs of individuals. However, this brings responsibility, and I need to judge when to take something to supervision. Recognising my limitations and the boundaries of my role informs that decision. I am supervised by a clinical psychologist with a wealth of experience in psycho-oncology; she allows me to push the boundaries of my role skilfully. We have built up a relationship which allows me to feel safe within supervision and she is mindful, as I am, of when external pressures are building.

Working in psycho-oncology brings the unfortunate reality of supporting people whose lifespan is potentially shortened. Since I have been working in oncology for over 30 years advances in treatment mean that this is often not the case. However, in UM patients there are currently no proven efficacious treatments for metastatic disease. This is a difficult aspect of the role when patients come into the service. Furthermore, it has become more apparent during the COVID-19 pandemic that patients' distress has been compounded by the inability to plan and 'enjoy' the life they have left. I need therefore to be aware of the emotional and psychological toll of working with distress on myself and allow time and space to process and reflect on my interactions with patients.

Future role of Health Psychology in clinical practice

There seems to be a gap that Health Psychologists can fill between the clinical teams and indeed the clinical psychologists. Specialist nurses, while they are very psychologically aware, but with increasing demands on their time, do not have the training to deliver emotional and psychological support some patients need. Clinical psychologists deliver therapy, but it may be that a course of therapy is not needed. A Health Psychologist can assess the nuances of distress given the context of the patient and decide what level of psychological support if any is needed. This 'triage' approach early on may help alleviate pressures on mental health services. Having one embedded within specialist teams gives immediate access to theoretically informed psychological assessment and early brief intervention if needed with the potential to prevent future distress. So often patients have been put on waiting lists for overstretched psychology services. I would like to see Health Psychologists playing a larger part in physical health care but especially in patients with cancer.

Conclusions

My research and clinical role are closely integrated. Much of my work role has been seen as a 'laboratory' to test out theory and frameworks to inform clinical practice. This, I hope, will benefit patients with cancer generally to help them cope with the consequences of living with a cancer diagnosis and an uncertain future. I hope in this chapter I have built a coherent picture of my role that has been challenging and rewarding in equal measures and hope it will inspire future Health Psychologists.

References

Brennan, J. (2004). *Cancer in context: A practical guide to supportive care.* Oxford: Oxford University Press. https://doi.org/10.1002/pon.1027.

Brennan, J. (2001). Adjustment to cancer – coping or personal transition? *Psycho-Oncology,* 10 (1)1–18https://doi.org/10.1002/1099-1611(200101/02)10:1<1:aid-pon484>3.0.co;2-t.

Brown, S. L., & Salmon, P. (2019). Reconciling the theory and reality of shared decision-making: A 'matching' approach to practitioner leadership. *Health Expectations,* 22(3), 275–283. https://doi.org/10.1111/hex.12853.

Brown, S. L., Hope-Stone, L., Heimann, H., Damato, B., & Salmon, P. (2018). Predictors of anxiety and depression 2 years following treatment in uveal melanoma survivors. *Psycho-oncology,* 27(7), 1727–1734. https://doi.org/10.1002/pon.4715.

Brown, S. L., Fisher, P. L., Hope-Stone, L., Hussain, R. N., Heimann, H., Damato, B., & Cherry, M. G. (2020). Predictors of long-term anxiety and depression in uveal melanoma survivors: A cross-lagged five-year analysis. *Psycho-Oncology,* 29(11), 1864–1873. https://doi.org/10.1002/pon.5514.

Cook, S., Salmon, P. & Damato, B. (2008) Reflections on developing a routine psychological assessment service for patients with uveal melanoma. *Health Psychology Update* 17(1), 56–61.

Cook, S. A., Damato, B., Marshall, E., & Salmon, P. (2011). Reconciling the principle of patient autonomy with the practice of informed consent: decision-making about prognostication in uveal melanoma. *Health Expectations,* 14(4), 383–396. https://doi.org/10.1111/j.1369-7625.2010.00639.x.

Cook, S. A., Salmon, P., Hayes, G., Byrne, A., & Fisher, P. L. (2018). Predictors of emotional distress a year or more after diagnosis of cancer: a systematic review of the literature. *Psycho-oncology,* 27(3), 791–801. https://doi.org/10.1002/pon.4601.

Damato, B. (2001). Detection of uveal melanoma by optometrists in the United Kingdom. *Ophthalmic and Physiological Optics,* 21 (4), 268–271. https://doi.org/10.1046/j.1475-1313.2001.00595.x.

Damato, B. (2010). Does ocular treatment of uveal melanoma influence survival? *British Journal of Cancer,* 103(3), 285–290. https://doi.org/10.1038/sj.bjc.6605765.

Damato, B., & Heimann, H. (2013). Personalized treatment of uveal melanoma. *Eye*, 27(2), 172–179. https://doi.org/10.1038/eye.2012.242.

Damato, B., Eleuteri, A., Taktak, A. F., & Coupland, S. E. (2011). Estimating prognosis for survival after treatment of choroidal melanoma. *Progress in Retinal and Eye Research*, 30(5), 285–295. https://doi.org/10.1016/j.preteyeres.2011.05.003.

Doherty, C., Stavropoulou, C., Saunders, M. N., & Brown, T. (2017). The consent process: Enabling or disabling patients' active participation? *Health*, 21(2), 205–222. https://doi.org/10.1177/1363459315611870.

Elwyn, G., & Miron-Shatz, T. (2010). Deliberation before determination: The definition and evaluation of good decision making. *Health Expectations*, 13(2), 139–147. https://doi.org/10.1111/j.1369-7625.2009.00572.x.

Fisher, P. L., Salmon, P., Heffer-Rahn, P., Huntley, C., Reilly, J., & Cherry, M. G. (2020). Predictors of emotional distress in people with multiple sclerosis: A systematic review of prospective studies. *Journal of Affective Disorders.276*, 752–764https://doi.org/10.1016/j.jad.2020.07.073.

Fisher, P., & Wells, A. (2009). *Metacognitive therapy: Distinctive features* (vol. 1). Abingdon: Routledge.

Folkman, S., & Greer, S. (2000). Promoting psychological well-being in the face of serious illness: When theory, research and practice inform each other. *Psycho-Oncology*, 9(1),11–19https://doi.org/10.1002/(sici)1099–1611(200001/02)9:1<11:aid-pon424>3.0.co;2-z.

Hoerger, M., Scherer, L. D., & Fagerlin, A. (2016). Affective forecasting and medication decision making in breast-cancer prevention. *Health Psychology*, 35(6), 594. https://doi.org/10.1037/hea0000324.

Hope-Stone, L., Ablett, J., & Salmon, P. (2019a). Reflections on a Health Psychology Service for Patients with Uveal Melanoma: The Challenge of Psychological Screening and Intervention When Distress is 'Normal'. *Journal of Clinical Psychology in Medical Settings*, 26(4), 421–429. https://doi.org/10.1007/s10880-018-9595-2.

Hope-Stone, L., Brown, S. L., Heimann, H., & Damato, B. (2019b). Comparison between patient-reported outcomes after enucleation and proton beam radiotherapy for uveal melanomas: a 2-year cohort study. *Eye*, 33(9), 1478–1484. https://doi.org/10.1038/s41433-019-0440-0.

Hope-Stone, L., Brown, S. L., Heimann, H., Damato, B., & Salmon, P. (2015a). Phantom eye syndrome: patient experiences after enucleation for uveal melanoma. *Ophthalmology*, 122(8), 1585–1590. https://doi.org/10.1016/j.ophtha.2015.04.005.

Hope-Stone, L., Brown, S. L., Heimann, H., Damato, B., & Salmon, P. (2015b). How do patients with uveal melanoma experience and manage uncertainty? A qualitative study. *Psycho-oncology*, 24(11), 1485–1491. https://doi.org/10.1002/pon.3813.

Hope-Stone, L., Brown, S. L., Heimann, H., Damato, B., & Salmon, P. (2016). Two-year patient-reported outcomes following treatment of uveal melanoma. *Eye*, 30(12), 1598–1605. https://doi.org/10.1038/eye.2016.188.

Jim, H. S., & Jacobsen, P. B. (2008). Posttraumatic stress and posttraumatic growth in cancer survivorship: a review. *The Cancer Journal*, 14(6), 414–419. https://doi.org/10.1097/ppo.0b013e31818d8963.

Kujala, E., Mäkitie, T., & Kivelä, T. (2003). Very long-term prognosis of patients with malignant uveal melanoma. *Investigative Ophthalmology & Visual Science*, 44(11), 4651–4659. https://doi.org/10.1167/iovs.03-0538.

Lazarus, R. S., & Folkman, S. (1984). *Stress appraisal and coping*. New York: Springer.

Nordin, K., Berglund, G., Glimelius, B., & Sjöden, P. O. (2001). Predicting anxiety and depression among cancer patients: a clinical model. *European Journal of Cancer*, 37(3), 376–384. https://doi.org/10.1016/s0959-8049(00)00398-00391.

Peters, E., McCaul, K. D., Stefanek, M., & Nelson, W. (2006). A heuristics approach to understanding cancer risk perception: contributions from judgment and decision-making research. *Annals of Behavioral Medicine*, 31(1), 45–52. https://doi.org/10.1207/s15324796abm3101_8.

Pilnick, A., & Dingwall, R. (2011). On the remarkable persistence of asymmetry in doctor/patient interaction: A critical review. *Social Science & Medicine*, 72(8), 1374–1382https://doi.org/10.1016/j.socscimed.2011.02.033.

Salmon, P. (2000). *Psychology of medicine and surgery: A guide for psychologists, counsellors, nurses and doctors*. Chichester: Wiley.

Schwab, A. P. (2006). Formal and effective autonomy in healthcare. *Journal of Medical Ethics*, 32(10), 575–579.

Shontz, F. C. (1975). *The psychological aspects of physical illness and disability*. London: Macmillan.

Sinding, C., Hudak, P., Wiernikowski, J., Aronson, J., Miller, P., Gould, J., & Fitzpatrick-Lewis, D. (2010). 'I like to be an informed person but…' negotiating responsibility for treatment decisions in cancer care. *Social Science & Medicine*, 71(6), 1094–1101. https://doi.org/10.1016/j.socscimed.2010.06.005.

Singh, A. D., Turell, M. E., & Topham, A. K. (2011). Uveal melanoma: trends in incidence, treatment, and survival. *Ophthalmology*, 118(9), 1881–1885. https://doi.org/10.1016/j.ophtha.2011.01.040.

Swindell, J. S., McGuire, A. L., & Halpern, S. D. (2010). Beneficent persuasion: techniques and ethical guidelines to improve patients' decisions. *The Annals of Family Medicine*, 8(3), 260–264. https://doi.org/10.1370/afm.1118.

Virgili, G., Gatta, G., Ciccolallo, L., Capocaccia, R., Biggeri, A., Crocetti, E., … & EUROCARE Working Group. (2007). Incidence of uveal melanoma in Europe. *Ophthalmology*, 114(12), 2309–2315. https://doi.org/10.1016/j.ophtha.2007.01.032.

Vodermaier, A., & Millman, R. D. (2011). Accuracy of the Hospital Anxiety and Depression Scale as a screening tool in cancer patients: a systematic review and meta-analysis. *Supportive Care in Cancer*, 19(12), 1899–1908. https://doi.org/10.1007/s00520-011-1251-4.

Watson, M., White, C., Lynch, A., & Mohammed, K. (2017). Telephone-delivered individual cognitive behavioural therapy for cancer patients: An equivalence randomised trial. *Psycho-oncology*, 26(3), 301–308. https://doi.org/10.1002/pon.4338.

Watson, M., White, C., Davolls, S., Mohammed, A., Lynch, A., & Mohammed, K. (2013). Problem-focussed interactive telephone therapy for cancer patients: a phase II feasibility trial. *Psycho-Oncology*, 22(7), 1485–1491. https://doi.org/10.1002/pon.3194.

Wells, A. (2011). *Metacognitive therapy for anxiety and depression*. Guildford: Guilford Press.

Zigmond, A. S., & Snaith, R. P. (1983). The Hospital Anxiety and Depression Scale. *Acta psychiatrica scandinavica*, 67(6), 361–370. https://doi.org/10.1111/j.1600-0447.1983.tb09716.x.

5 A spectrum of applied Health Psychology

Across public health and healthcare practice

Lisa Newson

I am a Health Psychologist …

- … a reader in applied Health Psychology
- … a lecturer, an academic
- … a researcher
- … a clinician, AKA practitioner psychologist
- … a health professional

I have experience and expertise in …

- … clinical interventions
- … public health, programme management
- … health commissioning
- … consultancy projects
- … teaching and training
- … qualitative and quantitative research (including grant writing and article publishing)
- … policy and strategy development, implementation and evaluation.

My research and clinical interests span …

- … diabetes (primarily Type 2)
- … obesity
- … coronary heart disease
- … health improvement

These topics include prevention and treatment and seek to incorporate the psychological needs and perspective of users/patients/clients into services and interventions.

DOI: 10.4324/9781003120469-6

I am a Health Psychologist with multiple 'hats' and proud not to be in a box, defined and restricted by a job title. I have the flexibility to engage across disciplines and be creative about what, how, and why I get involved in a project. My work is applied: developed within or transferred back typically into public health and healthcare practice, which enriches the patient and public experience, enhances health delivery and improves clinical outcomes. During my career, I have received plenty of knock-backs and challenges, but this has made me stronger, better able to position my skills and sell my profession for its unique and variable approaches.

When asked what I do, I identify and refer to myself as a Health Psychologist. However, technically I have never had the job title 'Health Psychologist' (although I have been recruited because I am a Health Psychologist).

In my early career, I would insert 'Health Psychologist' into job search engines and become frustrated that people and organisations were not advertising for Health Psychologists. In the early days I was so enthusiastic about promoting Health Psychology, I did not realise how niche our profession was. Talking to public health professionals about behaviour change and models of individual health behaviour influencing a wider population health model was, back then, a bit 'out there', and they were not convinced I was offering something they did not know already. Psychological, mental health professionals such as cognitive behavioural therapists and clinical psychologists whom I approached or worked alongside wondered how a Health Psychologist could offer the service users something which they did not or could not. The art of being a Health Psychologist has been to learn how to sell my skill without freaking out those around me, reassuring that they were not engaging with an unknown profession. In this sense, I have been a bit of a chameleon, adapting to the needs of those I work with (non-health-psychology colleagues), to blend into the environment (department/service) to achieve my job objectives, and be part of the team, but to enhance where able and add-value. That is how I have created my profile as a Health Psychologist.

The following provides some insight into the roles I have completed and the experience I have gained. In part, this varied experience was encouraged by completing the professional doctorate training (in 2008) and the need to demonstrate a range of competencies and skills.

Prior to commencing my training as a Health Psychologist, I worked on clinical-research projects employed within university and NHS settings. I conducted various research activities with clinical populations, which gave me insight into both the academic world and the clinical environment. This work included talking to patients and their families, listening to their stories and experiences of an illness and how the services were supporting them; working alongside various health professionals and learning about the challenges associated with providing services, and NHS red tape.

In development

My first 'trainee' Health Psychology post was as an applied researcher. I was employed at a university as a health behaviour specialist for an action research project, designing, implementing and evaluating a childhood obesity service to a clinical population as part of a commissioned pathway between the local hospital provider, the local council and the university. This was an excellent, creative and varied role, which felt like more of an intervention placement than research. This role allowed me to develop and train in various intervention techniques. Of particular interest to me at this time was applying solution focused brief therapy in obesity treatment. Working with both children and their families in an action research project encouraged growth for both the service users and for me. The application of psychology into this work was diverse and at times I drew on concepts from art therapy and creative activities to engage children in specific psychological techniques. A key aspect of this role was collaboration and working with other health professionals, taking our skills and knowledge, considering the evidence and implementing sessions, which made a change and helped the families deal with the 'label' of their child living with obesity. Within this role, I built some understanding of commissioning service requirements and the strategic pressures placed on a health intervention to perform and demonstrate positive clinical changes.

During my training, I also worked in a clinical psychology NHS service (initially, the post was for a higher assistant psychologist and then re-banded to a trainee psychologist), primarily supporting adult (and older adult) clients. I would select those clients most suited toward Health Psychology rather than mental health referrals. For this, I received CBT clinical supervision and applied my training to a range of clients over a 12-month period, and this position also served as an intervention placement for my trainee portfolio. I built therapeutic alliances mostly through one-to-one working although also conducted group interventions focusing on eating behaviour or health-related anxiety. Working together with my clients to formulate and work through sessions was extremely rewarding, and continuing to develop, reflect and refine my clinical skills was a central part of my development as a Health Psychologist.

However, it was very apparent to me that clinical psychology services, by nature, were set up to support mental health but staff were expected to deal with all and anything that was within their (broad) inclusion criteria. At the time, the majority of staff were unfamiliar with the concept of Health Psychology, so if they saw an opportunity to pass on a health-related client, they were quick to come and find me. This was a great opportunity; however, the lack of commitment and direct support to becoming a Health Psychologist (and not pursuing the clinical psychologist training route) was disheartening, even though I *was* in training. In addition, I observed the pressure and stress endured by the staff in the service and wondered if this was what the NHS had to offer, and if being in a clinical-psychology service was the best place for a Health Psychologist.

During this placement, my post was split to work within cardiac rehabilitation, alongside a clinical psychologist. The clinical psychologist provided supervision, although it was noteworthy that the clinical psychologist had no formal training in cardiac rehabilitation, and we built a mutually beneficial working relationship sharing clinical and Health Psychology practices and techniques. I thrived within this cardiac rehabilitation environment, offering one-to-one, group-based interventions and supporting the clinical staff through mentoring and training in psychological understanding and techniques.

However, I was aware that as the only person from a Health Psychology background being employed within a mental Health Psychology-based service was limiting, and long-term, if I was going to make a difference and get a full-time position within a health-focused role, I would have to influence the programme directors and/or commissioning practices.

In my opinion, the benefit of job advertisements not listing a '(trainee) Health Psychologist' is liberating in that it opens up the job market. Advertisements that requested a skill set and sparked an interest were exciting to me. (While I do hope that more posts for Health Psychologists/practitioner psychologists are advertised in future, I also do not want our profession to be boxed into the only titled jobs for specific grades at specific times of the year. This, for me, would have been limiting, and I do not want us to lose our varied and open opportunity to work with all.)

While training, I deliberated on my skills and development and recognised my competency base was to include training health professionals. I applied for a job as a 'health promotion training co-ordinator', a band above my trainee pay. To my surprise, I got the job, I did not sell myself as a trainee Health Psychologist, but all my skills were promoted. I stood out, I 'offered something more', more than the current stop smoking advisors who had applied or the health promotion manager for the area, or the nurses who wanted a training role. I stood out, and this was because I nailed the integration of Health Psychology models, techniques and methods into my interview process. This was a great role. I was able to design, develop and deliver various training packages, resources and toolkits to staff across all aspects of health, from health promotion in the workplace through to health management in clinical settings. Across my work, I implemented Health Psychology evidence, theory and approaches into the learning packages. I helped to change service operations and improve the functioning of staff within their roles. I gained further knowledge of strategic and operational functioning across services and built relationships with clinical staff through management and administration, all of whom helped me grow and understand how Health Psychology was relevant and needed (across primary, secondary, community and social care services).

Qualified Health Psychologist

I was targeted for promotion and moved into public health, first as a senior health development officer (covering obesity and health trainers). Subsequently, upon completion of my training period, when I became eligible for both chartership with the British Psychological Society (BPS) and registration with the Health and Care Professions Council (HCPC), I was promoted to commissioning and programme manager for healthy weight and public mental health (noteworthy here due to the range of experience; my pay grade was significantly beyond that of my peers just qualifying as clinical psychologists). Unfortunately, these roles no longer exist, and commissioning and programme management has been split into contracting and commissioning, service delivery, and implementation management. However, for me, this experience shaped my career, bringing all my expertise and knowledge together.

My work focused on utilising knowledge and evidence to understand the population needs and profile services and interventions. I initiated research and evidence-building projects, worked up new strategies and pathways, and collaborated with various internal and external stakeholders, managing various interventions and services. My expertise within public health was highlighted as exemplary by the Department of Health (DoH) and recognised within *Strategic High Impact Changes: Childhood Obesity* (DoH, 2011). As lead author of the Healthy Weight Strategy, I successfully directed 18 objectives and 67 projects (covering obesity prevention and treatment). The DoH acknowledged my documents as 'the most comprehensive pathways we have seen to date with frontline staff demonstrating a good understanding'. I designed these new pathways for equality impact, using profile mapping of prevalence, deprivation, and insight segmentation on family clusters to ensure that services responded to the needs of specific social groups (a unique methodology adding social value). I applied return on investment (ROI) modelling for the treatment of childhood obesity and implementation of prevention pathways and calculated significant financial savings per year. This ROI modelling subsequently released finance for the development of my National Child Measurement Programme (NCMP) pathway, which initiated 400+ new referrals/year for children identified as overweight or obese (who otherwise would not have received any intervention). While clearly the description of my role here was led by public health, and I received additional training on broader skills (such as ROI), ultimately my passion, commitment and high standard of work was informed and led, in my opinion, by my Health Psychology competencies, evidence-base and skills.

It is noteworthy that during this role I started to build a portfolio of evidence for the submission to become a registered public health specialist (to get the recognition within public health, because I wanted it but not because I relied on it). While things got in the way, and I did not pursue this, I strongly believe that Health Psychology has crossover and complementary competencies, and for those Health Psychologists working in public health, dual-registration should be an option (or indeed portfolio submission for retrospective recognition, should be supported and recognised; see below for more commentary on this).

Alongside my role in public health, I also continued to engage in clinical practice, supporting patients with obesity and diabetes, maintaining my clinical skill and working with those in need. Again, when appropriate with skills and experience, I strongly support Health Psychologists working within clinical services. To do so, we need to, externally, promote and sell our skills to those involved in service management (operational) and design (commissioning), and internally within psychology, provide supervision and support new trainees to have therapeutic and intervention skills appropriate to work with patients across a range of health conditions and contexts.

When the government planned to move public health into the local authorities, I felt uncomfortable being employed by an organisation essentially driven by politics and aware I was about to lose flexibility and variety in my job. I wanted to be able to remain influential and driven by my skill. At this point, I reflected on my career development and acknowledged that I wanted (for the first time) to work with other Health Psychologists and get involved in the profession, motivating new talent and more people to become Health Psychologists. I joined academia, as a senior lecturer in psychology, at Liverpool John Moores University (LJMU) which had an established and professionally accredited MSc in Health Psychology.

An academic

Until recently, I have struggled with the concept of being an 'academic'. I have developed my career primarily within the NHS and clinical environments, supporting patients with various health conditions. I have trained thousands of health professionals and taught on various degree courses, having gained the Higher Education Academy (HEA) teaching recognition. Academia has been an organisation, but not my definition, for that my identity has remained as a Health Psychologist who continues to engage in wider projects but brings along and supports others (students) into the profession. However, as a lecturer, I have taught across various psychology-based programmes, and my passion for applied psychology is transferred to students through my teaching across levels 4–8. I supervise students and encourage innovation to develop projects with external partners such as in the NHS, schools, charity and commercial sectors. My work, and that which I encourage students to engage, creates public insight developing new intervention approaches or aims to change practice.

For the last six years, I have been the MSc Health Psychology programme leader. This role is all-encompassing, including a student facing role, managing the programme, the modules and the students' needs, alongside the academic and administrative elements associated with a professional-body-accredited postgraduate course. I believe that my programme leadership adds social value to the university and to the public. Many MSc Health Psychology alumni are employed in Health Psychology-related sectors enriching the lives of individuals and communities through knowledge transfer (e.g. NICE; NHS, public health, third sector, or other academic institutions). My esteemed Health Psychology colleagues have developed the Professional Doctorate in Health Psychology, which allows students to complete the professional training route to become Health Psychologists, for which I am part of the team and provide supervision to trainees. I have, at present, supervised eight students to level-8 award and currently support four others. My supervision has resulted in all of my level-8 students conducting research and interventions of social and cultural benefit. For example, together, we have conducted public community workshops and transferred new knowledge to develop practical training for healthcare. I am also a supervisor for the BPS stage-2 independent training route and a national assessor for the qualification. I have conducted 12 Level-8 national examinations and additional internal and external examinations (e.g. PhD viva voce; professional doctorate examiner). Supervising, mentoring and examining trainees' development to become Health Psychologists of the future (or a psychologist with interests in health, for those who are PhD graduates) is one of the most rewarding aspects of my role.

I engage in research (through undergraduate, masters, PhD, professional doctorate and independent projects), and my core approach is applied in nature- to make a change, to inform policy, practice, or the lived experiences of those impacted. I have projects exploring prevention and public health initiatives around diet (e.g. Abayomi et al., 2020; McCann et al., 2018) and physical activity (e.g. Owen et al., 2019; Trapasso et al., 2018) through to treatment approaches for diabetes and obesity (e.g. British Psychological Society, 2019). Most recently I have published articles relevant to the management (Patel et al., 2021; Gibson et al., 2021) and prevention (Vaja, et al., in press) of type 2 diabetes, integrating the consideration of Health Psychology into patient experiences. A traditional academic is bound to the process of research outputs. However, my focus combines research with impact, ensuring that research is applicable to the real world, and can be used to inform and change services. I have expertise in qualitative methods, although will engage in quantitative analysis when required. I do not restrict myself to 'topics', but I am open to broad opportunities if I can see the value of Health Psychology. This keeps me busy and in demand, and allows to me to keep developing and bringing new ideas to the table.

Knowledge exchange

Alongside my research, I continue to act as a clinical practitioner and maintain intervention and therapeutic skills. I also participate in a range of additional stakeholder and consultancy activities, which involves supporting conferences and developing collaborations with strategic health partners. I engage outside of the arena of Health Psychology and promote our profession into health more generally. I collaborate and support colleagues in nursing and specific services in the NHS. I have conducted various consultancy projects all promoting and linking Health Psychology, and when able, I try to build Health Psychology capacity into these project experiences for a new student, a trainee placement or a more substantial long-term post, such as within the new long-term condition pathways which NHS Improving Access to Psychological Therapies (IAPT) services implement. I have influenced policy and support the development of our professional body, the British Psychological Society. Most recently, as a member of the PsychoSocial Aspects of Diabetes (PSAD) study group (part of the European Association for the Study of Diabetes) I have contributed to the PSAD response (Speight et al., in press) to the recent publication made by the *Lancet* Commission on Diabetes (Chan et al., 2020). We as the PSAD welcomed the *Lancet* report, although further highlight the need to recognise the role of psychology within diabetes care (specifically acknowledging issues of diabetes distress).

Becoming a reader and the future

At the beginning of 2020 I submitted my profile and CV for consideration of conferment to reader. I submitted under the route of social and economic engagement, often referred to as 'engaged scholar'. Award via this promotion route acknowledges outstanding contributions to social and economic engagement and impact through commercial enterprise, knowledge exchange, cultural activities, underlying scholarship and professional activities that have a significant positive impact for the university and wider society. For this process I had to demonstrate my work was recognised nationally, and the external reviewers of my application would have to agree I fully achieved the outlined criteria to be awarded promotion at this level. I submitted my application for review in February 2020, at which point I had 104 outputs from a varied portfolio of work. These outputs included academic research publications, conference articles, and professional, strategic and policy documents. Until this point I had been awarded £177,000 in research funding. However, in my opinion, some of my biggest achievements were the changes in practice made by health professionals following my input, and the ROI cost-savings achieved to improve healthcare services and pathways. In December 2020 I was notified of a successful promotion outcome (delay in process due to COVID-19, backdated to August 2020), and at this point I became a reader in Applied Health Psychology.

During the COVID-19 2020–2021 restrictions, I was adversely affected in my working practice, with IT difficulties, home-schooling, young children and health concerns. At the time, I felt very unproductive (a consequence of very high expectations), though on review while I was not as active as usual, I had still been busy. Throughout 2020, I continued to attend to both my teaching and MSc programme leadership duties, and in addition worked up a number of grant applications and additional publications. I have also continued to engage in national developments, such acting as a policy representative for British Psychological Society on childhood obesity, to support the development of a briefing document by the UK Parliamentary Office of Science and Technology (February 2021).

My work with the NHS continues and I am very keen to push psychological approaches further into obesity and diabetes services, though I have also been invited into projects for Cardiovascular and liver disease. I am currently collaborating with a CVD group, engaging with researchers and clinicians across the UK and internationally (New Zealand), and my obesity work includes collaborations in Brazil. In the Northwest of England, I have taken forward the role of deputy chair of ARC NorthWest Behavioural Sciences group, which seeks to bring together expertise within academia and healthcare for future collaborations. During 2021, I am acting as guest editor for a special edition (Biological and Psychological Aspects of Diabetes and Obesity) within the *International Journal of Environmental Research and Public Health*, which is seeking to consider alternative approaches and strategies in the prevention and treatment of obesity and diabetes.

I continue to collaborate with various external organisations including charity, NHS, and local authorities, for which I offer added-value to their teams through a Health Psychology perspective contributing to the improvement of individual's health. In the past year I have secured funding for a student bursary, and also additional research funding to connect and evaluate building sensors in homes, so that I can start to develop a person-home-behaviour profile, in the context of public health improvement. In January 2021, I was informed of a successful outcome to a Management Knowledge Exchange Partnership (mKTP) application for a two-year funded project to unite Liverpool-based housing association Cobalt Housing, Innovate UK and LJMU. This innovative project, 'Healthy Homes – Healthy Tenant – Healthy Community', will seek to advance organisational culture and to improve the quality of life of tenants in north Liverpool. We are focusing on health and wealth creation for tenants, for their communities, and for Cobalt as an organisation. Within LJMU I have established a team across schools and faculties, including colleagues from Liverpool Business School, School of Built Environment and the Data Science Research Centre, together in one collaboration that covers multiple strands of tenant, community, regeneration research and innovation. This is an exciting yet challenging mKTP, given its multi-disciplinary nature, and is one of the first in the UK and the first in LJMU's history, as the project is led by a Health Psychologist within the School of Psychology (until this project only Business Schools have been awarded mKTP funding). This project will direct my Health Psychology focus back towards public health applications, seeking to investigate determinants of health and design interventions to improve both health and behaviours for individuals and communities.

The future of Health Psychology

It is noteworthy that during the COVID-19 pandemic that Health Psychologists have been instrumental in supporting the immediate and ongoing national response (Arden, Byrne-Davis, Chater, Hart, McBride & Chilcot, 2020; McBride, Arden, Chater & Chilcot, 2021). Health Psychologists have advised on the prevention of transmission (e.g. physical distancing and social contacts, mask wearing and hand washing behaviours); they have been involved in symptom identification and behaviours for self-isolation; vaccine uptake; managing illnesses, and adaptations to the new normal. Specifically, the British Psychological Society, COVID-19 Behavioural Science and Disease Prevention Taskforce, led by the Division of Health Psychology Chair, have recently published guidance for the public regarding COVID vaccination (British Psychological Society, 2021); guidance for 'Delivering effective public health campaigns during Covid-19' (British Psychological Society, 2020a); plus specific guidance to encouraging healthy behaviour during the COVID-19 pandemic, focusing on the topics of alcohol consumption (British Psychological Society, 2020b), eating behaviour (British Psychological Society, 2020c), physical activity (British Psychological Society, 2020d), sedentary activity (British Psychological Society, 2020e), sleeping behaviour (British Psychological Society, 2020f), stopping smoking (British Psychological Society, 2020g), and additional guidance encouraging self-isolation to prevent the spread (British Psychological Society, 2020h).

I highlight the role of behavioural science, specifically that of Health Psychology, within public health and healthcare management, as demonstrated above through the COVID-19 response Health Psychologists have added significant value to public health management of the pandemic. Qualified Health Psychologists demonstrate competencies, skills and knowledge across a comprehensive syllabus; many of these overlap with those outlined within the public health skills and knowledge framework. Health Psychologists with applications in this field should be recognised for their expertise and experience in techniques, context and delivery of public health outputs. Similar to a GP who may apply for specialist Certificates of Eligibility for Specialist Registration (CESR), this route should be considered further for Health Psychologists, and I encourage the BPS to actively revisit and pursue this as a development for the professional. Alternatively, the portfolio submission for retrospective UKPHR specialist registration could be supported and recognised. I welcome the actions of fellow Health Psychologists, who are working with Public Health England and Health Education England to establish funded opportunities for Health Psychologists in training (Bull, Newman, Cassidy, Anderson & Chater, 2020) who can support population health improvement (Watson, 2020), this indeed is a positive development, but we are at the tip of the iceberg, and if we genuine want to improve and change health in our population, public health need to embrace Health Psychologists further.

Moreover, with specific reference to Health Psychologists in healthcare: the role of psychology within health and social care has been recognised, most noticeably by NHS England who, in December 2019, published a document for consultation entitled *Psychological Professions Vision for England 2019–24*, which aims to acknowledge and maximise the impact of psychology into the NHS Long Term Plan. The BPS welcomed this document and submitted a consultation response outlining the support for further integration of psychology into the NHS long-term but also raised several points for clarification and enhancement within the document itself (British Psychological Society, 2020i). The final version of the NHS England document is yet to be published.

Moving forward on this agenda and in recognition of the value for psychologists within health and social care, the BPS released guidance regarding the best practice for recruiting Practitioner Psychologists (which includes Health Psychologists) into applied health and social care settings (British Psychological Society, 2021). Historically Clinical Psychologists have held the majority of health-based positions, primarily working within the mental health sector. However, the psychology sector has changed, alongside the changing needs of the population. Health Psychologists, have knowledge, skills and expertise across physical health conditions (within prevention and treatment), are recognised by the HCPC, and it is noteworthy that since 2020 NHS England now codes all as applied psychologists, and specific job roles are referred to as practitioner psychologists (within specialism, e.g. health, counselling, clinical etc.). I am fully supportive of these changes and believe that Health Psychologists have a unique and complementary offering within healthcare and as such should be embraced, further promoting the profession of the practitioner psychologist. That said, in-house at the BPS, recognition for funded places for trainees via NHS contracts should be prioritised for action, shared across the practitioner psychologist professions (to include health and counselling).

In summary

I am busy. Sometimes I take on too much. I sometimes work with other Health Psychologists, although often not. Many of my collaborations are with health professionals across disciplines, including but not limited to, dietetics, nutrition, physiotherapy, medicine, and public health. I work in academia, but this has not restricted my engagement activity, more so it has given me a broader platform. I am not *really* a chameleon (just when I need to be). I think Health Psychologists are more like panthers. An umbrella term for a variety of expertise and interests. We have an impressive knowledge and skill set, and we can add value, which other health professionals cannot. We are not a common allied health professional, which should be to our advantage (when we know how to make it so). I am a rounded professional proud of calling myself a Health Psychologist and able to explain the complexity and variation in what I, and we (as a profession) can offer. But this has been challenging to get here, not least because I have been finding my unique way, and 'sussing out' what I am good at, what I enjoy and of course what I am less keen doing, but learning how to explain and sell myself, and feeling comfortable with doing so, given I don't fit into a box. I do not think Health Psychologists ever will: this is our charm.

At the heart of what I do is to improve experiences for those at the user-end of the topic. This can be: assessing health risks and seeking to reduce health inequalities across a population or community, working with the public to design, engage and evaluate health improvement interventions; it can providing psychological support for clients managing their long-term condition; it can be engaging research participants in and with the evidence I am developing; it can be students whom I motivate to become the Health Psychologists of the future. I am committed to developing and utilising the Health Psychology evidence base, implementing Health Psychology into practice wherever relevant. *Health Psychology is relevant to all*; to those who are ill and managing health conditions, to those who are healthy and wanting to stay so. Thus, Health Psychology is an exciting profession to be part of because it is relevant for every workplace, every organisation, healthcare prevention and healthcare treatment. Every public and private sector can employ and work with a Health Psychologist, and for that, I will continue to be adaptable and responsive to their needs, because I can, and I have some additional knowledge and skills. I love being part of a profession which is varied and unique, with so much to offer. Until recently I had not considered my profile and evaluated who I am as a Health Psychologist. I do what I enjoy and what I'm good at. I welcome newcomers into our profession, and I am open to new discussions or those seeking out information or support.

References

Abayomi, J. C., Charnley, M. S., Cassidy, L., McCann, M. T., Jones, J., Wright, M., & Newson, L. M. (2020). A patient and public involvement investigation into healthy eating and weight management advice during pregnancy. *International Journal for Quality in Health Care*, 32(1), 28–34. doi:10.1093/intqhc/mzz081.

Arden, M. A., Byrne-Davis, L., Chater, A. M., Hart, J., McBride, E., & Chilcot, J. (2020). The vital role of Health Psychology in the response to COVID-19. *Health Psychology*, 25(4), 831–838. doi:10.1111/bjhp.12484.

British Psychological Society. (2019). *Psychological perspectives on obesity: Addressing policy, practice, and research priorities*. Leicester: British Psychological Society.

British Psychological Society. (2021). Guidance following your first vaccination dose. Retrieved from www.bps.org.uk/sites/www.bps.org.uk/files/Policy/Policy%20-%20Files/Guidance%20following%20your%20first%20vaccination%20dose.pdf (March 2021)

British Psychological Society. (2020a). Delivering effective public health campaigns during Covid-19. November. Retrieved from www.bps.org.uk/sites/www.bps.org.uk/files/Policy/Policy%20-%20Files/Delivering%20effective%20public%20health%20campaigns%20during%20Covid-19.pdf.

British Psychological Society. (2020b). Covid-19 public health road map: Alcohol consumption. October. Retrieved from www.bps.org.uk/sites/www.bps.org.uk/files/Policy/Policy%20-%20Files/Covid-19%20Public%20Health%20Road%20Map%20-%20Alcohol%20consumption.pdf.

British Psychological Society. (2020c). Covid-19 public health road map: Eating behaviour. October. Retrieved from www.bps.org.uk/sites/www.bps.org.uk/files/Policy/Policy%20-%20Files/Covid-19%20Public%20Health%20Road%20Map%20-%20Eating%20behaviour.pdf.

British Psychological Society. (2020d). Covid-19 public health road map: Physical activity. October. Retrieved from www.bps.org.uk/sites/www.bps.org.uk/files/Policy/Policy%20-%20Files/Covid-19%20Public%20Health%20Road%20Map%20%E2%80%93%20Physical%20activity.pdf.

British Psychological Society. (2020e). Covid-19 public health road map: Sedentary behaviour. October. Retrieved from www.bps.org.uk/sites/www.bps.org.uk/files/Policy/Policy%20-%20Files/Covid-19%20Public%20Health%20Road%20Map%20-%20Sedentary%20behaviour.pdf.

British Psychological Society. (2020f). Covid-19 public health road map: Sleep hygiene. October. Retrieved from www.bps.org.uk/sites/www.bps.org.uk/files/Policy/Policy%20-%20Files/Covid-19%20Public%20Health%20Road%20Map%20-%20Sleep%20hygiene.pdf.

British Psychological Society. (2020g). Covid-19 public health road map: Stopping smoking. October. Retrieved from www.bps.org.uk/sites/www.bps.org.uk/files/Policy/Policy%20-%20Files/Covid-19%20Public%20Health%20Road%20Map%20-%20Stopping%20smoking.pdf.

British Psychological Society. (2020h). Encouraging self-isolation to prevent the spread of Covid-19 encouraging self-isolation to prevent the spread. July. Retrieved from www.bps.org.uk/sites/www.bps.org.uk/files/Policy/Policy%20-%20Files/Encouraging%20self-isolation%20to%20prevent%20the%20spread%20of%20Covid-19.pdf.

British Psychological Society. (2020i). British Psychological Society response to NHS England Psychological professions vision for England 2019–24. Retrieved from www.bps.org.uk/sites/www.bps.org.uk/files/Policy/Policy%20-%20Files/BPS%20Response%20-%20Psychological%20Professions%20Vision%20for%20England%202019-24.pdf.

British Psychological Society. (2021). Best practice in psychology recruitment. Retrieved from www.bps.org.uk/sites/www.bps.org.uk/files/Policy/Policy%20-%20Files/Best%20practice%20in%20psychology%20recruitment.pdf.

Bull, E., Newman, K., Cassidy, T., Anderson, N. & Chater, A. (2020) Reflecting on the Stage 2 Health Psychology independent training route: A survey of trainee and graduate experiences of employability. Retrieved from https://uobrep.openrepository.com/bitstream/handle/10547/624807/Stage2independentroutefinal.pdf?sequence=2&isAllowed=y.

Chan, J. C., Lim, L. L., Wareham, N. J., Shaw, J. E., Orchard, T. J., Zhang, P. & Gregg, E. W. (2020). The Lancet Commission on diabetes: using data to transform diabetes care and patient lives. *The Lancet*, 396(10267), 2019–2082. doi:10.1016/S0140-6736(20)32374-32376.

DoH. (2011). *Strategic high impact changes: Childhood obesity*. London: DoH.

Gibson, B., Umeh, K. F., Newson, L., & Davies, I. (2021). Efficacy of the best possible self protocol in diabetes self-management: A mixed-methods approach. *Journal of Health Psychology*, 26(3), 332–344. doi:10.1177/1359105318814148.

McBride, E., Arden, M. A., Chater, A., & Chilcot, J. (2021). The impact of COVID-19 on health behaviour, well-being, and long-term physical health. *British Journal of Health Psychology*. doi:10.1111/bjhp.12520.

McCann, M. T., Newson, L., Burden, C., Rooney, J. S., Charnley, M. S., & Abayomi, J. C. (2018). A qualitative study exploring midwives' perceptions and knowledge of maternal obesity: Reflecting on their experiences of providing healthy eating and weight management advice to pregnant women. *Maternal & Child Nutrition*, 14(2), e12520. doi:10.1111/mcn.12520.

NHS England (2019) Psychological professions vision for England 2019–24. Retrieved from www.england.nhs.uk/publication/psychological-professions-vision-for-england-2019-24/.

Owen, M., Kerner, C., Newson, L., Noonan, R., Curry, W., Kosteli, M. C., & Fairclough, S. (2019). Investigating adolescent girls' perceptions and experiences of school-based physical activity to inform the girls' peer activity intervention study. *Journal of School Health*, 89(9), 730–738. doi:10.1111/josh.12812.

Patel, T., Umeh, K., Poole, H., Vaja, I., & Newson, L. (2021). Cultural identity conflict informs engagement with self-management behaviours for South Asian patients living with Type-2 diabetes: A critical interpretative synthesis of qualitative research studies. *International Journal of Environmental Research and Public Health*, 18(5), 2641. doi:10.3390/ijerph18052641.

Speight, J., Hermanns, N., Ehrmann, D. on behalf of the PsychoSocial Aspects of Diabetes Study Group of the European Association for the Study of Diabetes (in press). Data on diabetes-specific distress are needed to improve the quality of diabetes care. *Lancet*.

Trapasso, E., Knowles, Z., Boddy, L., Newson, L., Sayers, J., & Austin, C. (2018). Exploring gender differences within forest schools as a physical activity intervention. *Children*, 5(10), 138. doi:10.3390/children5100138.

Vaja, I., Umeh, K. F., Abayomi, J. C., Patel, T., & Newson, L (in press). A grounded theory of type 2 diabetes prevention and risk perception. *British Journal of Health Psychology*. doi:10.1111/bjhp.12503.

Watson, D. (2020). How will you help to sustain collective efficacy? Retrieved from https://thepsychologist.bps.org.uk/how-will-you-help-sustain-collective-efficacy.

6 Beating your imposter syndrome to become a practitioner Health Psychologist

Koula Asimakopoulou

Introduction

This chapter recounts my experience of becoming a Health Psychologist. Starting from a PhD in 'something that resembles cognitive psychology but with people with diabetes' all the way to setting up a private practice, the chapter hopes to show how you can grow and develop in health, on a journey to becoming a scientist-practitioner.

An accidental encounter with a discipline that was 'never going to take off'

Picture this: a teenage girl, exploring relationships. She thinks she would really like to have an encounter with a partner who is tall, fit, Mediterranean-looking, probably an extravert, who is young, a little loud, the life and soul of a party. Someone who enjoys the summer, sand, sea and sangria, and being carefree. Someone who is confident and self-assured. The sort of person you would see on advertisements promoting cool perfume, sexy aftershave or designer jeans. That person! Imagine also that our character has been observing, for some time, other girls dating this type of partner and feels that this seems 'the right one' for her.

Then imagine that, after some effort, she meets someone who broadly matches this profile. He is a true extravert, Mediterranean and athletic, loves the beach, adores sangria and is truly care-free. Confident and self-assured, he seems to be exactly the sort of person she was hoping to meet. They meet while on holiday and they spend time together. They find out about each other, they get to explore what each other likes and loathes. But, somehow, there is something missing. Somehow, although he 'ticks all the boxes' he does not seem to be the perfect partner she had imagined. She cannot quite put her finger on what it is that does not seem quite right. He is a Mediterranean beach and party-lover … but not quite what she had in mind. She

DOI: 10.4324/9781003120469-7

decides not to rush, take some time to think through the relationship. And while she is doing this ... she bumps into someone who certainly does not tick any of the boxes she had set up for herself when looking for a relationship; because he is not that tall, and certainly not that fit. He is blonde, quite reserved, and has more of a Scandinavian profile. He is certainly not carefree; more of a quiet, introverted person who prefers winter sports to sunny beaches. Shy and unsure about himself, he is still working out what he wants from life. And somehow, although he has none of the features she thought she was looking for in a relationship, somehow, she knows, he is 'the one'.

Although this is a tried and tested scenario for 'rom-coms', it is also how I found Health Psychology. Or rather, how Health Psychology found me. Because when I first encountered Health Psychology, I did not know I had found my life partner, nor had I aspired to spend all my life with it! Rather, being convinced that I probably wanted to be a clinical psychologist (the sporty Mediterranean partner), I 'fell' into the arms of Health Psychology (the quiet, introverted northern European) rather unexpectedly.

Health Psychology found me when I was offered a scholarship to work on some doctoral research at the University of Surrey a year after I graduated with a first-class honours degree in psychology. Having spent a year as an assistant psychologist in a clinical psychology department doing research with two rather different groups of people (people with agoraphobia and people who had deliberately self-harmed), something did not feel quite right. I was in a clinical psychology department, working within the NHS, 'helping people' who were offered reliable psychotherapy methods to change life for the better.... This is precisely what I had aspired to do, this is exactly what I had dreamt of when I turned down the party invitations in my third year of my degree and chose to stay in and revise! This was pure and simple clinical psychology research, so this should have ticked all my boxes. And somehow, it just did not feel right. Was it the bureaucracy associated with working in a hospital setting? Was it the particular patient groups that did not quite feel 'clinical' enough? Was it the type of therapy offered to these people? It was not clear what was wrong, but something clearly did not sit well. And while these thoughts were all-consuming, I decided that it was time to re-evaluate the clinical psychology dream and look at other areas of psychology. It was at this point that I was lucky enough to be offered a scholarship to do a PhD working in physical (diabetes) rather than mental health; here I was going to work with people with type 2 diabetes and explore how the illness impacted on cognitive function and how such an impact was related to people's attempts to self-manage the illness. This felt really quite exciting. So I was moving away from clinical populations, but still staying with patients. I was moving away from mental health, but not too far, in physical health. And this was now going to allow me where I would want to be in psychology, later on in life. So, at first this was very much a Scandinavian winter-sports potential partner crossing my path while I was re-evaluating my relationship with the Mediterranean beach party enthusiast who had not turned out to be all that I had imagined him to be. Unbeknown to me, that was my introduction into Health Psychology. And I am so glad I decided to take the plunge and explore an area that, on first impressions, did not meet any of the needs I thought I had.

This was in 1995. And I remember to this day, 25 years later, the words of my clinical psychologist colleague as I was leaving the world of deliberate self-harm and agoraphobia to take up a PhD in diabetes: 'Patients with diabetes are the hardest ones to work with, you know. You will struggle to recruit them into research.' This was a totally erroneous statement – I have found working with people with diabetes a complete and totally rewarding experience, where participants were as keen to help me with my research as I was to try and understand how diabetes impacted on their lives. But, although an inaccurate prediction, what this statement was totally predictive of was the difficulty that some psychologists would have in welcoming Health Psychology, this new kid on the block, into the family of established psychology disciplines.

I started my PhD in the mid-1990s in what was 'no man's land' in terms of area of expertise that I was going to be working in. Put simply, when I started I did not know this was my first step towards a career in Health Psychology. Because at that time, although there were rumours and rumblings about 'psychology as applied to medicine', 'behavioural psychology in health settings' and other similar descriptors, Health Psychology in the UK was only just forming as an idea and as a Division – the BPS Division of Health Psychology was only set up in 1997. So, leaving clinical psychology research work behind, I was really walking into the unknown. I was going to work on a PhD on 'Cognitive function in people with type 2 diabetes; implications for diabetes self-management'. But other than a clear title, there was not much else that was clear in terms of what discipline I was working in or where it sat within mainstream psychology.

I remember, starting to work on this PhD and having to justify to colleagues what I was doing – but failing to do so in a clear or convincing way. So, I was obviously not training to become a clinical psychologist because I was not on a clinical doctorate and the work I was going to be doing was not in mental health. I was not a cognitive psychologist because although I was using cognitive testing, I was using these tests only as a tool to make conclusions about people's illness management, rather than assessing from a purely cognitive perspective. And then, where I was looking at how people with diabetes recalled their dietary and exercise health behaviours and fitted those decisions in personal and social life, I could not really call myself a social psychologist, because again, I was 'borrowing' social psychology tools to explore health behaviours. This felt a little like a PhD where I was 'fudging' pure social and pure cognitive psychology and I was hoping not to be found out, a feeling that often still plagues me! A few years into my PhD, the Division of Health Psychology was formed. And then, all of a sudden, my work had a home. I was not a 'sort of ... kind of a cognitive psychologist'. Nor was I 'something like a social psychologist but not really, interested more in diabetes than social psychology'. I had a home of my own in that I was using broad psychological principles from various, traditional, well-established fields of mainstream psychology, to better understand health and illness in people with type 2 diabetes. And then I knew, that my Scandinavian, not quite self-assured, winter-sports-loving, but also needing time to find himself partner had a name. He was a Health Psychologist – and we had stumbled into finding each other.

Going back to the rom-com script, it is often the case that when girl meets boy, there is often resistance from family and friends. There was certainly no resistance that I encountered in calling myself a Health Psychologist, from neither family (who to this day still, sadly, think I am a clinical psychologist ...) nor friends (most of whom are fellow Health Psychologists). The resistance came from colleagues with expertise in traditional, mainstream psychology disciplines. The number of times I described myself as a Health Psychologist only to be told that 'Health Psychology is a fad' or 'you know this will never take off' is shockingly high. But reflecting on it, it really did not affect any of my decision-making or how I felt about Health Psychology. To me, my professional identity was clear; there were no questions as to whether what I was doing was Health Psychology. I was clear what and who I was, and I was really passionate that I could now call it what it was – Health Psychology was a discipline in itself, that while others might have needed time to accept it, I was quite happy that it fully described the work I was doing.

So when I completed my PhD in 2001, having moved from a full time to part-time PhD to take up a post as a lecturer in psychology (note the absence of 'Health' from the title!), I knew I was graduating with a PhD in *Health* Psychology. That was despite my degree certificate, like my job title, also omitting the 'Health' from the title! Health Psychology was taking off, but the world around it was going to take a little time to accept it. So when the opportunity arose to become chartered with the BPS as a Health Psychologist through the 'grandparenting' route (a route that recognised a variety of health work that was likely to had been accumulated in the absence of formal branding of it as 'health'), I leapt at it; I became a chartered Health Psychologist in 2001 as soon as I had completed my PhD and then registered with the Health Care Professions Council as a practitioner psychologist some years later, when that became a requirement for psychologists seeking to apply psychology in practice.

From academic work to becoming a practitioner Health Psychologist – first steps and hurdles

I spent a large part of my working life employed as an academic Health Psychologist. From my first lectureship in psychology in the mid-1990s, I moved to my first lectureship in *Health* Psychology at the University of Bath in 2000 while in the final stages of my PhD, and I was employed to teach on the Bath MSc in Health Psychology. Since then I have moved academic departments, but always stayed in posts where 'Health Psychology' was very obvious and always a part of the job title. As part of this journey I had the great pleasure of working with some great colleagues in the UK and abroad and to have invested time contributing to the academic development of the discipline as part of, among others, the BPS Division of Health Psychology Training Committee and the BPS Division of Health Psychology Executive Committee. Having supported Health Psychology at various academic departments in the UK and abroad, I found what has been a home in 2007 at King's College London, where I have been employed as an academic Health Psychologist to work with dental teams, bringing the world of Health Psychology to dentists' and patients' journeys.

While at King's, and while the post was primarily research and teaching-based, the opportunity arose to do some clinical work in parallel, with people who were fearful of the dentist. There was an obvious difficulty here though; while I had developed sound academic skills in Health Psychology all this time, while I knew about personal models of illness, illness representations and basic behaviour change ideas, I had not had the chance to become trained in what seemed to be the 'go to' skill set to help people with a fear of the dentist. This is where my journey on adding clinical skills to my toolkit started with some basic courses in cognitive behavioural therapy (CBT).

Shortly after that, the first ever psychology service for people with dental fear was set up at Guy's Hospital in London and I found myself really enjoying the quick rewards that work with dental patients brings – seeing applied psychology totally transform people's lives is an experience that stays with you for life. Really, words just cannot describe the immense feeling of reward and accomplishment that I have experienced seeing someone who, for example, has been too scared to walk past a dental surgery, having their teeth scaled and polished having totally conquered the fear of the dentist. That was just magic! And although some CBT principles and techniques were of use, there were broad, Health Psychological principles based on communication skills, psychoeducation, goal-setting and person-centred healthcare that all came together to help this patient sit in a dental chair. So this was, very much, Health Psychology at its best; doing what it did best (supporting people with health decisions such as attending the dentist) while using tools and techniques from other disciplines. But to get to this stage, there were a fair few obstacles to overcome. First, there was the obvious battle with the thought that 'this is dental fear; this is a mental health problem and you are thinking of using CBT; that is what clinical psychologists do; you are a Health Psychologist; so (i) you should really leave this work to the people who actually know how to do it and (ii) if you carry on, do hope you will not be found out'.

Health and clinical psychology have always overlapped to some extent, and probably always will. There is a long debate over boundaries between the two disciplines and what each one should and should not engage with. For a really sound historical overview of how Health Psychology emerged and how it sat alongside clinical psychology, do have a look at Quinn et al. (2020). But for now, it is worth noting that dental fear could be seen as a mental health issue – that Health Psychologists should not interfere with, or it could be seen as a health behaviour (avoiding the dentist, forgoing receiving essential health care, non-adherence with advice to visit a dentist) that is entirely up a Health Psychologist's street. So, the dilemma of whether this is really Health Psychology will always be there, where there are two disciplines with some degree of overlap between what we do and where there are health behaviours that need addressing. But I have to confess that although I have heard numerous Health Psychologists question their skill set and think thoughts similar to the one I outlined above, never, as in, not once, in my entire working life have I heard a clinical psychologist wonder whether they have the skill set to help support patients with physical health concerns! I shall leave the reader to make what they will of this statement!

So, the first hurdle to overcome in this journey was my own thought processes about the legitimacy or not of my work as a Health Psychology practitioner. The second issue to contend with was that of other healthcare professionals and how they saw Health Psychology as a discipline. In my experience, there are clinicians who *totally* see what Health Psychologists have to offer and others who find it a little more difficult. The clinician who is familiar with Health Psychology tends to see it as a science where we use tried and tested, evidence-based theory and methods to help people deal with, manage and respond to health and illness impacts. They tend to see us as a partner to what they do – someone with a skill set that complements their work; for such a clinician, it is obvious that, for example, you can be the world's most accomplished dentist at root canal treatments, but where the patient is too concerned to come and sit on your dental chair, then you cannot quite do your world-leading root canals so you may need a Health Psychologist to help. Or, in cases where you fit the most wonderful braces to achieve the most fantastic straight teeth, none of this will happen unless your patient adheres with your advice once they have left the surgery. This, then is very much a case of a partnership between dentistry and Health Psychology where the two co-exist and complement each other. It would be as pointless to ask the skilled endodontist to support behaviour change in a dentally fearful patient, as it would be to ask me as a Health Psychologist to do root canal work on a patient. And where we all understand each discipline's strengths, this makes for a really happy co-existence. But then, there are other healthcare professionals who struggle to see what Health Psychologists do. I still remember a discussion I have had with a senior manager, who greeted my excitement at the proposal of offering Health Psychology support to fellow staff and students with the comment, 'But I need you to apply for grants and do research, I do not pay you to be an agony aunt'. There is still a lot of misunderstanding out there as to what practitioner Health Psychologists can do, which can be a hurdle to practising Health Psychology. In my personal journey, views such as this did become a bit of a stumbling block that meant that having been part of the first year or so of the very successful dental psychology service at Guy's I was pulled back to do research, grant-writing and teaching, as per the academic contract that I was employed to fulfil. Despite my enforced pull back to teaching and research, and as is often the case in life and in rom-coms, the girl-meets-boy story can have a happy ending though, even with the hurdles I have described above; the Health Psychology service for dental fear at Guy's is doing well, being headed up by not one but two Health Psychology practitioners.

My venture out into private practice – building an independent Health Psychology practice

As must be obvious so far, practising as a Health Psychologist in my mainstream work was a fruit I was allowed to taste but not allowed to carry on sampling for long. At the same time, the rewards of Health Psychology practice were so great and so impactful that the idea of not practising, simply because it was not in the interests of an academic employer to allow me to do so, seemed odd. My jump into private practice was very much a combination of push and pull factors; a disillusionment with the world of chasing grant money and the challenges of teaching clinicians certainly felt like pushing forces, forces that gave me the strength and resolve to create opportunities for private practice work. And then, the powerful memories of 'that feeling' when you see a fellow human being change for the better as a result of your joint work, using Health Psychology research theory and evidence, pulled me into thinking about the possibility of private work.

It took around a year of working through unhelpful, self-defeating thoughts ('Am I good enough? Will I be 'found out'? I am a real psychologist? Can I do this solo? Do I have enough therapy skills? But I am not a businesswoman! What if patients complain?') and putting the decision off before, in the summer of 2017, I took my first steps as an independent practitioner Health Psychologist, setting up the Mind Umbrella, an independent Health Psychology practice in Kent. Getting to that stage involved several behaviours that aimed at dealing with my unhelpful thoughts above and taking practical steps to set up the practice.

The first step, and really probably the building block of the endeavour, was to seek advice and knowledge on how to set up a psychology practice. A true academic at heart, I read about it (Bor & Stokes, 2011) and then, having decided that this all sounded very good but it was all probably going to be just too hard, I decided not to set up until I really knew what this was going to look like. As must be obvious by now, the 'you are not good enough' story is one I often tell myself, so it took me a year of digesting Robert and Anne's book content AND looking to add to my therapy skills, before I took the leap. To the latter end I enrolled in several CPD courses, mainly round updating my core skills of CBT; you will find there are several BPS-approved providers who deliver this sort of training. I took a year-long course on third wave CBT approaches; then, having been really impressed with the wonderful world of acceptance and commitment therapy (ACT), I enrolled on a few online courses to really hone my skills in this domain. Over the years I have been making a point of enrolling into at least one CPD course on clinical skills. Compassion-focused therapy has been another one area I have really enjoyed furthering my skills in.

So, after a year of thinking about it then deciding against it, and having read the book, I took Robert Bor's 'How to set up a Private Practice' one-day training in London. That was really what finally made me believe that I should have a go – seeing a room full of other psychologists asking the very same questions as I did. If you were thinking of setting up in private psychology work, and you are thinking of doing one course to help you, this course is the one to do!

So, over a year now of thinking about it, reading about it, going on courses to deal with the 'but you do not know what you are doing' syndrome, worrying that I may not have all the skills necessary or the business acumen to do it, then worrying about the ethics behind the idea of charging anyone to talk to me (another self-defeating strategy that clearly does not feature in the minds of other professionals from builders to lawyers!), I took the plunge. I decided it was time to see if I could set up a private practice. Here, a lot of CBT-based techniques were really helpful; asking myself what is the worst that can happen if I try it and fail, what would be the best that could happen and what would be most likely to happen, gave me the springboard to make the next move.

The second step after attending Robert's course that was the most influential was to find a person to support building a website and create a brand name. I was very lucky to find a brilliant professional who took her time to guide me through the process, put up with all my changes of mind from the most important things (what are we going to call the practice) and registering it, to the tiny details (which shade of lilac should we use for the logo).

Running a practice and being a solo Health Psychology practitioner

Having dealt with the practicalities of setting up the practice, finding clinic space, getting insured, complying with the various bodies that regulate practice and so on (GDPR and ICO), I found myself actually being a Health Psychology practitioner, with a website, access to a clinic space and referrals (mainly from word of mouth, local advertising and then, later on, from health insurance companies). So it did not happen overnight. It took about a year or two to move from the occasional, couple of referrals a month to a steady suite of 6–10 clients at any one time. But as this was very much an add-on to my 'real' academic post. It is fair to say that this work has been the most rewarding, exciting, worthwhile activity I have engaged in, all my working life. It gives me opportunities to have an impact on people's lives; it serves as a test-bed for some of the most popular Health Psychology theories; it gives me a chance to put into practice the theories and work that I have been researching or lecturing about for over 20 years. And the rewards are quick; on average, six sessions with a client can see them move from the grips of depression or anxiety to a healthy, values-driven, healthier life. Although most people present to me because of difficulties with mood (arguably a clinical psychologist's patch), you will find that a lot of the time the depression or anxiety is the result of behaviours that are generally unhealthy. Supporting behaviour change with unhealthy behaviours deals with those behaviours which then has a long and substantial impact on the client's depression and/or anxiety. You can have for example, a person with diabetes who is depressed. You can ask a clinical psychologist to treat the depression. Or, you can use illness representations and distress work to help the person self-manage their diabetes; with the latter, you change their health behaviours *and* the depression. Tackling only the depression seems rather superficial. Examples such as this serve as a reminder of the power of what we do as practitioners, the impacts we can have on people and the sheer opportunity that being a practitioner Health Psychologist provides to put all these skills into practice.

I hope that it is obvious at this point that there are some great aspects of private practice; you can choose the areas of Health Psychology you can work with and pass on to colleagues those cases that you are less interested or expert in. You get to 'travel' with your client, on their journey to a healthier, better life. When you get there (and most of the time you do get there), the feeling of accomplishment and satisfaction and success that your client experiences is something that they are almost always very happy to share. I can think of one example of a young man, who was going through a difficult time, his relationship with his partner having gone wrong and the family having broken up. He was referred to me because of persistent low mood. 'Severely clinically depressed' was the label. Scratching the surface, it was true that he was presenting with depression, but that was the outcome, not the cause of his problems. The cause of his problems was difficulties in forming or maintaining behaviours that would support the building of healthy relationships. After six sessions of simple behaviour change work to help him create a life he would prefer, the depression moved from 'severe clinical depression' to 'normal' on the Hospital Anxiety and Depression Scale (HADS; Zigmond & Snaith, 1986). The client seemed to now have developed healthier lifestyle habits. All seemed well. So when this client arranged his seventh session, several weeks after we had finished working together, I was a little perplexed. I thought we had finished? Why was he coming back? I arranged the session a little concerned about what we might discuss. When I asked him about an agenda for the session, he said:

> No agenda, today, because there is no need to. I am feeling on top of the world, I have cracked this. So I took the session because I just wanted to come and see you to tell you just how great this has been and how well I feel now.

It is moments like these that make private practice work so very rewarding.

But it is not all reward and fun, and often you do feel lost and it is good to discuss things with a clinical supervisor. Key to ensuring success with private practice is finding yourself a clinical supervisor that you feel comfortable with. It is important that they are practitioners themselves in an area that you plan to practise and that you feel comfortable talking to them. There are lots of colleagues out there who offer clinical supervision and, for me, it took a couple of attempts until I found someone that I feel I can ask the most 'stupid' questions, without feeling judged. So, in terms of setting up a practice, this is the third, most important step. Find yourself a supervisor who can help you grow as a practitioner and who is there to offer support and guidance while you are finding your feet.

Having said all the above ... private practice can have its tricky moments. Though these tricky moments are very, very rare, in my experience, they usually revolve around the feeling that you 'are not helping enough' for those clients with whom, regardless what you try, regardless how you formulate and attempt to tackle their concern, there seems to be little progress. Or, where once you think you have dealt with one issue, the client presents with another one, out of the blue, and usually totally unrelated to what they originally came to see you for, so the impression of 'lack of progress' is created (in your head, rather than the client's, I should add!). Or where you have been on a journey with the client, and then, suddenly, for no apparent reason, they disappear off the radar. These are very rare moments but they can feel odd, especially where the inner critic pipes up and hooks you with the 'You are not good enough' story.

Finally, a word of caution ... juggling understanding of Health Psychology as a science with practising it can be lots of fun, but it can also be exhausting. Keeping up with the latest developments in Health Psychology research is hard enough when you have an interest in a *single* Health Psychology area. Doing this for a wide range of areas, and practising at the same time, can be a tricky act to maintain. It is important that you do your best and accept that there will be occasions where you may well miss the key reference that was going to unlock the mystery of your client's problems! Science is forever moving forward and, as long as we are not too far behind, we can still do a lot of good.

Concluding thoughts

Overall, my journey in the discipline has been varied and spanning a great many areas. From an accidental encounter with the discipline, having always thought I wanted to be a clinical psychologist then a move into diabetes, then into dentistry, I have had the opportunity to research, teach, supervise and now practise a lot of Health Psychology. Practising has very much come as a Plan B for me; when going into my PhD, the plan was never to practise. I always saw myself as a researcher, an academic, a scientist, rather than a practitioner. And yet, having been a scientist for many years and getting the opportunity to practise as part of the dental fear service at Guy's, I sampled the rewards of practice, almost by accident. They were too rewarding to want to move away from practice. It was that experience that turned me from a scientist to a scientist-practitioner and while the opportunity is there, the plan is to carry on juggling both balls.

References

Bor, R. & Stokes, A. (2011). *Setting up in independent practice: A handbook for counsellors, therapists and psychologists*. London: Macmillan.

Quinn, F., Chater, A. & Morrison, V. (2020). An oral history of Health Psychology in the UK. *British Journal of Health Psychology*, 25, 502–518. doi:10.1111/bjhp.12418.

Zigmond, A.S. & Snaith, R.P. (1983). The hospital anxiety and depression scale. *Acta Psychiatrica Scandinavica*, 67(6), 361–370. doi:10.1111/j.1600-0447.1983.tb09716.x.

7 Health Psychology in a clinical setting
How it works for me

Jennifer Pulman

Introduction

When I look back to eighteen years ago when I was first introduced to the realm of psychology, I find a much younger, focused, and motivated version of myself sitting in an A level psychology classroom. You could see the excitement in my wide eyes, soaking up all the interesting concepts being presented to me. I was lucky. My A level psychology tutor was inspiring. This is where my journey to becoming a qualified Health Psychologist starts and I am honoured to share my story in this chapter of my experiences which led me into private practice. As a therapist my main interests lie in working closely with people who struggle with mental health conditions, people who have been diagnosed with a long-term health condition or have suffered an accident or injury and more generally, people who wish to change unwanted behaviour. This means I get to see a wide range of individuals within my clinic which makes for an ever interesting and varied career. In this chapter, I share my reflections of working in a clinical domain, from my very first client right through to running a successful high street clinic alongside a team of other self-employed therapists. I do hope you find it helpful.

My journey into Health Psychology

Following an intense two years at Runshaw College studying psychology, I embarked on the next stage of my education at the University of Central Lancashire in Preston (UK). At this point in my learning I had not yet come into contact with the field of Health Psychology; I had not heard of this branch until entering the third year of my psychology undergraduate degree. Throughout my degree I was aware, however, that in my third year I would have a choice to either stay routed to a single honours Psychology degree or specialise in a certain area of psychology. My initial

DOI: 10.4324/9781003120469-8

instinct was to specialise as I selfishly believed that this would help me stand out from the other 800 students who started studying psychology alongside me. Even at this point I was hell bent on becoming a psychologist, the type still to be determined. After a substantial amount of time perusing through all the module content across degrees, I opted to change my degree to applied psychology. This is where I came across the fields of work psychology and Health Psychology. Both appealed to me equally at the time. It opened up a world of fascinating topics which I would never have imagined been of interest to me before. Ergonomics was one of these. At one point I could see myself designing products for human comfort based on how we behave and view the world. I look back at this and laugh because I could not at the time, and still cannot, draw for toffee. But it was Health Psychology that won me over in the end. As I traversed through the different areas and applications, I quickly started to realise that I had much in common with Health Psychology. It took me back to high school when I had a battle with eating and body image issues; it resonated with my father who worked shifts all his life and struggled with stress, but most of all it appealed to my natural concern for the wellbeing of others. So, from here I knew that the pathway had been set, I was off to study Health Psychology at Masters level. There was just one problem. I flunked!

Well, not totally flunked. I ended up with a score of 59.4 per cent overall and I needed a solid 60 per cent to apply for the Health Psychology Masters course, otherwise known as Stage 1 training. If I could not get onto this course my career as a psychologist was pretty much over, so I believed at the time. I was never a first-class student; I really struggled to get good marks for my work in the first year of the degree. During the second year I worked hard at improving my scores and by the time I hit my third year they were improving dramatically. I finally understood how to write academically and write well. Overall, it just was not enough, and my previous year scores had dragged my average down. I was not to be defeated though, and I arranged a meeting with the lead on the master's course who assured me within ten seconds of my plea to be accepted that I would be. And I was! I made it, albeit by the skin of my teeth, to the next stage.

I found the masters course to be one of the most exciting and challenging times of my life. On my very first day of the course I was in a lot of physical pain due to having heart surgery. I had been diagnosed with third-degree heart block and had only just come out of hospital the week that my stage one training started. I remember the ice breaker during the first session clearly. A lecturer was throwing a beanie toy at all the students in turn and I couldn't catch it when it was my go because I could not raise my arm. It was at that point I had a feeling that this course was going to be tough. And it was. It seemed that an assignment was due in every single week since the course started; it felt relentless. At the same time it was fascinating as it opened up the whole new concept of behaviour change. So far in my training I had learnt all about how people behave and the reasons for it, but it was at this point I started to understand the different models of behaviour change, the barriers to change, how to design interventions and measure their effectiveness. Now this really caught my interest. I had always felt a deep need to help people feel better and I started to imagine a future where I could do this using all the knowledge I was taking in. It was an exciting time. One clear memory I have is standing in the room where all the student 'pigeonholes' were where our assignments were left for us to collect after having been marked. Every time I collected my work I used to glimpse over at the pigeonhole for PhD students and I remember thinking to myself that one day 'that would be me'. One day I would be collecting my mail and work from that very place. It was exciting times for other reasons as well. My masters research project focused on establishing a link between the 2D:4D ratio (a biological marker for *in vivo* testosterone exposure) and muscle dysmorphia (now more commonly referred to as body dysmorphic disorder) in men. I had the pleasure of visiting local body building gyms and measuring the fingers of the men who worked out there with the primary intention of their bodies becoming larger and stronger. I will never forget one gentleman who took part in my study saying to me 'this is a thing you know? This muscle dysmorphia thing' He looked around and told me 'nearly everyone here has it', then wandered off with a saddened expression. This was a turning point for me. It made me realise how much I wanted to work with people who had certain problems that were affecting their quality of life. I enjoyed collecting data, writing up the findings and presenting them, adding to the 2D:4D research base. But I knew this was not what I wanted to do as a career, I was destined to work to help people improve their lives. My interest in mental health now started to grow.

After completing the master's degree, I applied to Staffordshire University for the professional doctorate in Health Psychology, otherwise known as Stage 2 training. After a tricky start due to a serious lack of self-confidence I started to settle in well and get my head down. It was during the three and a half years I was on this course that I was introduced to consultancy work. Initially, this module was the one that scared me the most as I had no previous experience or knowledge in this area. It turned out to be the most inspiring and exciting module on the course. It sparked an immediate enthusiasm in working in self-employment and appealed generously to my business streak (I had been making and selling jewellery on eBay for some months at this point). My module leader filled me with confidence and encouraged me in my pursuit of becoming self-employed, working one to one with clients, learning how to coach and how to apply Health Psychology theory and models to a more clinical setting. Without his support I would not be where I am today; I have no doubts about that.

The world of work

When I first started studying at UCLan I was working as a support worker for adults who had a variety of different learning difficulties and personality disorders. This was an extremely rewarding five years but I also found it very challenging at times. I was assaulted on my first day with a swift slap across the back of head by a lady with schizophrenia. It was not enough to deter me from going back in the next day. My fondness for this particular lady grew and I know the feeling was mutual as I was informed by my colleagues that when I was not working in the home, she used to ask for me constantly 'Where's Jennifer? Where's Jennifer?' Over the years I worked with seven service users regularly and supporting these people in their day to day lives really helped me develop a deeper level of empathy for others. It's a trait that plays a huge part in my role now in my private practice and is usually commented on when my clients leave reviews.

At the time of starting the professional doctorate I was employed as an occupational therapy technical instructor (OTTI) at Blackpool Victoria Hospital. I primarily worked on the stroke unit which was my first experience of supporting people who were seriously physically and mentally unwell. It was a shock. I assisted people who were unable to sit up in a chair, people who were unable to communicate, people who were cognitively impaired and people who were heavily depressed. My role mainly involved carrying out assessments, both for physical and mental abilities and to work up close and personal with the patients to help them improve and recover. Sometimes the interventions worked and sometimes they did not. Sometimes after working very closely with patients, they passed away. These days were hard. But overall, I learnt so much from this role, from psychological assessments, (mood, cognitive, behavioural, quality of life assessments), to developing my communication, social, empathy and observational skills. I spent two years on this ward working within the National Health Service. It was a hugely valuable experience and I have no regrets, however it did eventually take a turn for the worse. The ward became a very stressful place to work and more and more colleagues from all areas on the stroke unit began to disappear. The pressure that I felt to meet the needs of the service, to give the patients what they deserved all became too much. I succumbed to a bout of work-related stress and became highly anxious about going into work. This was my first experience of anxiety and although it was a rough period of my life, it gave me a wider and more personal understanding of what it felt like to struggle with mental health. Shortly after this time I applied to work for the University of Liverpool as a systematic reviewer for the Cochrane epilepsy group.

Now this position was something else. Within my first week of employment, I was flown to Madrid for my very first conference. This was my first professional role which did not involve working directly with service users. Instead, I was sitting at a computer most days churning out systematic review after systematic review; I must have published over 50 papers over the four years I worked for the university. Even now, five years after leaving my position there, some of my work is still being published. I loved this job; it was truly amazing. It allowed me to travel to places all over the world, New Zealand, Canada and Spain, where I would have to present my most recent research findings. I had a good team around me, and it was lots of fun. However, there was this serious lack of client contact and after a while I was starting to miss working with people one-on-one.

At the same time, I was also employed as a volunteer assistant psychologist at a local hospital. This role allowed me to carry out my doctoral research projects among other assignments. Here I conducted focus groups with people with a diagnosis of cancer to examine levels of psychological distress which would inform the development of an intervention designed to help and support these people through their journey. Hearing people's stories was a privilege. When people opened up to me about their mental health and about the experiences they had been through I felt a huge sense of responsibility and just wanted to help them through it. It was at the point I started to research and train in therapeutic approaches. This placement ran throughout my doctorate programme and when I completed all my academic work the placement came to an end. I passed my doctorate and with the help and support of my supervisor I embarked on a new journey into the world of self-employment and consulting privately.

Setting up a private clinical practice

I remember my first client well. He called me 'fat' during our very first session. I thought I took it rather well, in fact I noticed how easy it was for me not to become offended by his remark. The fact that I was five months pregnant probably helped me react in a cool and collective manner and needless to say he was deeply embarrassed when I told him. It was this experience that made me realise this was where I was supposed to be. Funnily enough this client was referred to me by a psycho-legal rehabilitation company soon after I had qualified and registered as a Health Psychologist. I felt at the time I was not ready to take on private clients so I put the referrer off for two months stating I was busy. As it turned out, they waited for me. And two months later I was sat in a rented meeting room being called fat. Prior to this I had been working closely with my supervisor to build up my self-employed business on the marketing and promotional front. I started to design and build a website, I paid one of my artist friends to design a logo for me, I started to list my business in all sorts of places and promoted myself on social media. I also attended local business networking events and enrolled on a myriad of training courses, both business and psychology-related to develop my therapeutic knowledge and skills. Even after all the years of studying psychology, from A level to the professional doctorate it was becoming very clear that the learning never ends.

My private work began with one or two clients at a time for approximately a year and then my client base steadily started to grow. I did take up a teaching role at Edge Hill University which was part time so that I could stay working within an academic setting but pursue my career in clinical work at the same time. During this time I was renting a room at a holistic health centre on an ad hoc basis. It was called the Complementary Health Centre and it was managed by an acupuncturist who rented out rooms to other self-employed therapists. I used the room when I needed one to see my private clients; it was a straightforward arrangement and it worked. Until I started getting busier, that is. Over a couple of years I needed to use the room more; however, there were several occasions where there were none available and I could see this becoming to be a problem for me. As luck would have it, an opportunity came my way which I just could not decline. The acupuncturist who owned the centre was retiring and she offered me first refusal on taking over the clinic. After several conversations at home, with the previous owner and with my new landlord, I decided to accept and take on my first holistic clinic which provided a range of therapies including counselling, hypnotherapy and acupuncture. There were at least ten other self-employed therapists renting rooms through the week so I was taking all this on as well as my own private work. It was an exciting time for me and I really felt I was making moves in the right direction. After a year managing the clinic, I decided to change the focus of the clinic from providing holistic therapies over to talking therapies, and so the Talking Therapies Centre was born. Several therapists had already left the centre and we now had a team of therapists who mainly worked in mental health such as a child and adult counsellors, psychotherapists, hypnotherapists and of course myself providing psychological therapy.

My clinical work

As mentioned earlier, I work with a variety of people who have certain issues such as mental health problems or long-term health conditions. Sometimes these clients are referred to me from external organisations via an insurance claim. These people have tended to have had an accident or injury or have been mistreated in some form either by health professionals or during childhood. They may be struggling to cope with chronic pain, or other conditions such as tinnitus or fibromyalgia. Clients who approach me via my clinic or website are usually struggling with some aspect of their mental health; it may be stress-related, anxiety, depression, self-esteem or motivational issues. Sometimes these clients have been through a major health event which has triggered such feelings such as a heart attack or cancer. Sometimes people do not understand why they feel the way they feel. Regardless of the reasons why people seek psychological therapy, they will all go through a similar process shown below.

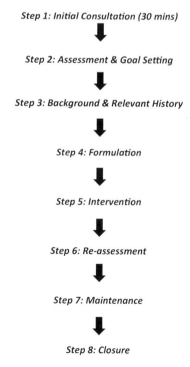

Figure 7.1 Process of client work

Each potential client attends a consultation prior to starting any therapy to briefly assess the main issues they are facing and whether they are a good fit for psychological therapy and their potential level of engagement. The client is allowed time to discuss their reasons for seeking therapy and notes are taken throughout. If they opt to begin a course of therapy, during their first session they will sign a contract outlining expectations of the therapeutic alliance. This covers issues such as confidentiality and anonymity. We will then discuss goals for therapy which are all assessed subjectively to determine how close a person is already towards achieving these goals. This, alongside other more formal assessments, provide a baseline to work with so that symptoms and goals can be monitored for progress over the course of therapy. The assessments clients will complete are dependent on their reasons for therapy and presenting symptoms or behaviours. A common mental health assessment would be the PHQ-9 (Kroenke et al., 2001), for assessing mood disturbance and GAD-7 (Spitzer et al., 2006), for symptoms of anxiety. Quality of life measures such as the WHO-QOL (Skevington et al., 2004), and self-esteem measures such as the Rosenberg Self-Esteem Scale (Rosenberg, 1989), may also be implemented. Other assessments which are designed to pick up on symptoms of specific health conditions or disorders may also be used as needed. I have used tinnitus questionnaires, post-traumatic stress measures, questionnaires for fibromyalgia symptoms, body image measures and others for identifying disordered eating patterns. There are many validated measures which can be used with one client; the key is not to overwhelm them during their first session but to introduce these measures at an appropriate time in their therapy journey.

Once a full history and background information has been gathered it is then time to establish with therapeutic approach to take with the client to help them achieve the goals they set out in their first session. This is wholly dependent on their presenting problem and what their therapy goals are. I tend to take a tailored approach to psychological therapy and may implement several approaches or a joint approach such as combining a cognitive behavioural approach and compassion focused approach. These are the two main therapy models I use with the majority of my clients. However, in some cases, such as car accident victims, I may utilise eye movement desensitisation reprocessing, otherwise known as eMDR. Often, I also teach mindfulness and meditation techniques for emotional management and for people who want to change behaviour I will mostly use motivational interviewing. Whichever therapy is selected, it is discussed in detail with the client so they know what to expect over the coming sessions. A formulation is also normally presented to the client after several sessions of gathering information. This covers significant historical events including upbringing, learning, traumatic one-off events or prolonged exposure to trauma, it also presents a client's core beliefs, key threats/fears, coping mechanisms, unintended consequences/behaviours and inner voice. This exercise allows the client to draw everything they have spoken out into an organised model where links can be established and understood with clarity. Most of my clients have found formulation itself significantly helpful; just having this knowledge and understanding of themselves can help to reduce some of the negative emotion surrounding them.

The duration of therapy is different for each individual, however usually I estimate anywhere between ten and fifteen sessions. Some people do not require this amount, and of course some require much more. This usually depends on the complexity of the presenting problems. During the course of intervention both myself and the client will monitor symptoms and re-assess at appropriate time points. Once symptoms start to diminish and the client feels they are drawing closer to achieving their therapy goals it may be time for them to enter the maintenance stage of therapy where they may begin to wean off therapy. A maintenance plan is carried out in a collaborative process and finally a closing session will take place to bring the therapeutic relations to a pleasant end. My role and the therapeutic process outlined above may appear to crossover into the realms of clinical psychology and in some respects it does. However, there are clear limitations to my role, and I know my boundaries. For example, I do not present a formal diagnosis of any condition. In fact, many clients who are referred to my services have already seen a clinical psychologist for a full psychological assessment with diagnosis prior to beginning therapy.

A large part of my role as a Health Psychologist involves teaching and training within my clinic. I am lucky to have a small group of passionate and enthusiastic volunteers and a psychotherapy placement student who I train and supervise in their roles. This involves sharing my knowledge of Health Psychology theory, models, research, assessment and intervention as well as aiding their understanding of psychological therapy. Their learning also involves shadowing me by sitting in on consultations and on rare occasions sitting in on a client session, with the client's consent of course. Alongside training I also engage in supervising some of my colleagues if they do not already have external supervision arranged. This usually involves a discussion of client progress, identifying key areas for exploration and helping people feel more confident in their role as a therapist. And, of course, I engage in my own supervision sessions at least once a month to reflect on my own progress as a psychologist and as a supervisor in line with the British Psychological Society (2018), and Health and Care Professions Council (2016) guidelines.

Developing the service

Over the six years I have been practicing as a Health Psychologist in private practice I have built up my client base to a place where I am now at full capacity. I have a small waiting list and so have a continuous flow of clients and some appointments held back for previous clients who wish to book in for a one-off session. This means that I am now in a position to help the other therapists who work with me to build up their client bases. This is mainly achieved through training my assistant psychologist to carry out a form of triage consultation and assess potential clients for the most appropriate type of therapy and most suited therapist. This is a collaborative process between client and assessor as I do believe that clients are the expert on themselves and are best placed, with a small amount of advice, to make the most appropriate choice. The clients who attend the clinic for the first time for their consultation are provided with information including the various types of therapy offered beforehand. Some people have clear ideas of the types of therapy that would be suitable and some do not.

Another way in which the services at the clinic are being developed is in the form of support groups and group classes. I started a male-only support group to encourage men to come along to the clinic and gain support for their mental health in a safe and comfortable setting. Over several months the group began to grow and the same faces turned up at most sessions. At first, I ran the sessions which included group psychoeducation and activities to encourage the men in the group to start opening up. Over time the group expressed their need to just talk to each other about core issues they were experiencing as opposed to learning, and so a new group facilitator took over. This was a counsellor at the clinic who was trained in group psychotherapy. This allowed me to focus on providing new classes which included topics such as mindfulness and meditation. These classes were very calming, and on a few occasions some of the clients fell asleep during the sessions rather than 'falling awake'. It was also very therapeutic for myself as it allowed me to relax at the same time as delivering the class.

Future services at the clinic include the development of a home-visit service for those people who struggle to attend the clinic for physical reasons or for people who experience extreme anxiety. Although there is an option currently to provide therapy at home via online services, some people do prefer face-to-face communication, and this is something we would like to provide in the near future.

Conclusion

Without a shadow of a doubt the work I do as a Health Psychologist is extremely rewarding. It is a real honour to bear witness to the stories of the people who come to see me in clinic for whatever reason. To be trusted with this personal information and to help people overcome their problems is a privilege. Although my clients learn from me as I help them through their therapy journey and work collaboratively towards the goals they wish to achieve, I equally learn from them. My clinical role with the Health Psychology domain is stimulating and full of variety. I always knew I wanted to work in a therapeutic setting one-to-one with people rather than in academia. Although there is some training on doctorate programmes focused on therapy or consultation it would be a brilliant move forward for this to have more of a focus within doctorate training and encouraged more within the field of Health Psychology as a whole. It is perfectly feasible for Health Psychologists to use their knowledge, skills and abilities to work within a clinical (mental health) setting and my role is a testament to this.

References

British Psychological Society. (2018). *Code of ethics and conduct*. Leicester: British Psychological Society.

Health and Care Professions Council. (2016). Standards of conduct, performance and ethics. Retrieved from www.hcpc-uk.org/globalassets/resources/standards/standards-of-conduct-performance-and-ethics.pdf.

Kroenke, K., Spitzer, R., & Williams, J. (2001). The PHQ-9: validity of a brief depression severity measure. *Journal of General Internal Medicine*, 16(9), 606–613.

Rosenberg, M. 1989. *Society and the adolescent self-image*, revised edition. Middletown, CT: Wesleyan University Press.

Skevington, S., Lofty, M., & O'Connell, K. (2004). The World Health Organization's WHOQOL-BREF quality of life assessment: Psychometric properties and results of the international field trial. A report from the WHOQOL Group. *Quality of Life Research*, 13, 299–310.

Spitzer, R., Kroenke, K., Williams J., & Lowe, B. (2006). A brief measure for assessing generalized anxiety: the GAD-7. *Archives of Internal Medicine*, 166(10), 1092–1097.

8 Assessment in Health Psychology clinical practice

Eleanor Bull and Hannah Dale

Introduction

Assessment is a core psychological intervention competency for Health Psychologists (Health and Care Professions Council, 2015), taught to doctoral level as part of Stage 2 Health Psychology Training programmes (British Psychological Society, 2015). Health Psychologists offer psychological interventions in many contexts to help people prevent illness, manage long-term conditions and improve the healthcare system (Johnston, 1994). Assessment goes hand-in-hand with formulation, discussed in the next chapter. Together they enable psychologists to gather and make sense of information to help reach a shared understanding of problems, which then guides intervention planning (Johnstone & Dallos, 2013).

Health Psychologists use their skills in assessment in a wide range of ways and settings. These are often with teams, communities, organisations or whole populations. For example, Health Psychologists often develop, deliver and evaluate public health interventions, conduct community needs assessments and coordinate asset mapping (Hussain & Knowles, 2020). In this way, assessing (and formulating) is vital to engage communities in healthy changes or co-design interventions to help healthcare teams change (e.g. Bull et al., 2019; Debono et al., 2017). For many Health Psychologists, their core work is within clinical health settings with people seeking psychological help within a healthcare system, whether to help prevent or self-manage long-term health conditions. In these contexts, Health Psychologists use assessment to guide their individual or group formulation-based psychological interventions. This would be in contrast to, for example, a protocol-based, manualised treatment often undertaken by allied health professionals or assistant psychologists. Assessment (and formulation) may also be used to facilitate shared decision-making or readiness for potential medical treatments such as bariatric surgery, or organ transplants, and in supporting multidisciplinary team colleagues to

DOI: 10.4324/9781003120469-9

work with individuals. Assessment is also essential for establishing whether the service will best meet the needs of the client and/or if we could help facilitate a referral to another service.

To our knowledge, there is no British Psychological Society (BPS) or Health and Care Professions Council guidance for assessment in Health Psychology clinical practice. Some critical Health Psychology colleagues argue that the 'social' is underrepresented in work with the biopsychosocial model by psychologists (Stam, 2015), including how to operationalise this in an assessment. We find that existing textbooks on psychological assessment (and formulation) tend to be organised with a primary focus on separate therapeutic modalities (e.g. Johnstone & Dallos, 2013; Parry, 2019). We find it useful to think more integratively about what is helpful across the broad settings Health Psychologists work within. Further, we have found that some therapeutic textbooks do not fully consider the complexities and individual differences in long-term health condition adjustment and self-management which characterises much Health Psychology specialist research and practice (e.g. Refsgaard & Frederiksen, 2013; Moss-Morris, 2013). For instance, one popular cognitive behavioural therapy (CBT) textbook claims 'two people with depression may have very different formulations, in contrast to two people with, say, lung cancer who wouldn't' (Townend & Grant, 2017, p. 8). Therefore, in this chapter, we aim to present a practical guide to Health Psychology assessment in clinical settings. We recommend reading it alongside our next chapter on formulation in clinical practice. In this chapter, we first describe our own experiences of Health Psychology assessment and the need we perceived for some extra guidance in this area. We then discuss integrative approaches to Health Psychology assessment, including typical areas discussed in a biopsychosocial clinical interview, common assessment measures and considerations for assessing risk in Health Psychology clinical practice.

There are many different terms for Health Psychology clinical services and the people they serve. In this chapter we refer to services to help healthy people keep well as 'primary prevention services' and services to help people adjust to, cope and manage acute or long-term conditions as 'physical health services' (sometimes these are referred to as clinical Health Psychology services). We refer to 'clients' rather than 'patients', even though the latter is still a commonly used term in healthcare. While the term client could be suggestive of a 'purchaser-provider' relationship (Nueberger & Tallis, 1999) we feel it helps to describe people playing an active role in their treatment and denotes a collaborative relationship which is vital in the work Health Psychologists do to help empower people.

Assessment in our roles as Health Psychologists

As practitioner Health Psychologists, we have been fortunate enough to develop our assessment skills while working in a wide range of health settings. We were some of the first trainees within the NHS Education for Scotland Trainee Health Psychologists scheme, undertaking Stage 2 training working in Scottish NHS public health settings on population and community-level behaviour change intervention projects, while developing, delivering and evaluating primary prevention services with adults from deprived areas and looked after children. Post-qualification, we have continued working on team and community level projects, while in our clinical work we have worked as Health Psychologists with children, young people and adults across the lifespan within a range of broad services and clinical specialties. This includes developing and refining our assessment (and formulation) approaches as Health Psychologists in primary care, sexual health and blood-borne virus, HIV, diabetes, paediatrics, hepatitis, oncology, acute and chronic pain management and substance misuse NHS physical health services. Our excellent psychology and multidisciplinary teams and colleagues have helped us shape our ideas about what may be common to most psychological professions and where our field tends to add expertise.

Assessment approaches in Health Psychology

The therapeutic traditions most commonly adopted by Health Psychologists in clinical practice (e.g. CBT; motivational interviewing, MI; acceptance and commitment therapy, ACT) tend to share an idiographic approach to assessment, aiming to understand a person's problems in terms of their personal meanings, experiences, motivations, thoughts, feelings and behaviours. This takes into account past experiences, historical and contextual issues and the full biopsychosocial range of factors influencing and maintaining people's problems. Unlike in nomothetic approaches (e.g. medical traditions), practitioner psychologists working in primary prevention and physical health services would not usually aim to classify people's experiences or 'symptoms' into aggregated disorder classifications, for example diagnosing adjustment disorders or mental health disorders in their assessments (unless there is a specific clinical benefit to doing so). The extent to which diagnostic labelling is helpful and valid in general remains a controversial topic within psychology and medicine (Watson, 2019). The challenge of living with long-term physical health conditions are such that for many conditions, clinical levels of anxiety and low mood are almost the norm rather than the exception (Psychological Professions Network, 2020). The idea that this represents a 'disorder' is problematic and can be unhelpful where people may already feel 'othered' because of their long-term condition. However, we find it vitally important to fully explore emotional health in our assessment and helping people tease apart the effects of their medical condition(s) and emotional distress (e.g. low energy levels) can be helpful and validating for people (Monaghan et al., 2010).

In some services such as paediatric clinics or inpatient settings, observation, home or school visits and interviews with family members or carers are possible and can be hugely enriching to a psychologist's assessments (and formulations). However, the standard, most common approach taken in adult outpatient services is the clinical interview, integrated with standardised self-report measures and health information from medical records. Therefore, below we discuss practical considerations surrounding conducting clinical interviews. A further important consideration is the risk of implicit bias introducing potentially discriminatory assumptions based on interrelated factors including ethnicity, sex and socio-economic status (Pickersgill, 2020). Psychologists should be aware of these, how such intersectionality might influence our assessment (and therefore formulation) and use supervision to explore potential biases where appropriate. For a comprehensive overview of intersectionality and health inequalities, we recommend Mullings & Schulz (2006).

Clinical interviews

In this section we discuss the typical sections and practicalities of clinical interviews, using a fictional case study of Anita, introduced in Box 8.1.

Box 8.1 Case vignette: Anita

Anita is a 61-year-old lady who had a myocardial infarction (heart attack) four months ago. She was treated with coronary angioplasty (with a metal mesh stent to widen her coronary artery). She was referred to the Health Psychology cardiac service by one of the team physiotherapists who said she was not engaging well in her rehabilitation programme as, although she attended appointments, she appeared anxious and fear-avoidant. While not sure at first about seeing a psychologist, Anita then said she would like help coping with the after-effects of her heart attack, especially with the fear that it's going to come back at any time.

Preparation

In primary prevention and physical health services, clinical interviews typically follow a semi-structured format, with open questions on key topic areas, with flexibility to be guided by the client and a focus on building empathy and rapport. A thorough understanding of available multi-disciplinary information is needed beforehand. In our experience, it is time well spent to plan for 1–2 hours before an assessment reading available hospital records or multidisciplinary team letters, understanding recent referrals or clinical results (e.g. viral load for a client with HIV), and discussing with team members to gain a wider picture. Where a Health Psychologist is new to a service or establishing a new service, it is key to ensure they understand the remit and service model (see our chapter on formulation).

Skills for engaging

In busy clinical practice settings, many factors may limit assessment session lengths, such as clients' concentration abilities, room availability or service agreements. During clinical interviews, psychologists therefore need to be able to gather much important information relatively quickly, while establishing a collaborative relationship. A challenge often experienced in physical health settings is engagement and expectation setting; often clients may have little or incorrect information about the psychologist's role. Some may worry that they have been signposted or referred to the psychologist because their professional team thinks their physical health problem is 'all in their head'. Sometimes, clients may not even be aware or remember that a referral has taken place or may not have fully consented. From our experience, we find it essential to spend a good deal of time during assessment empathically eliciting expectations. With permission, we can then provide normalising information about the psychologist's role in helping clients make difficult changes and/or cope with the normal challenges of living with a health condition.

This can be vital for correcting misperceptions and facilitating engagement: a short example of this process is in Box 8.2.

Box 8.2 Engaging clients in a Health Psychology assessment

PSYCHOLOGIST: So, Anita as I mentioned, I'm the Health Psychologist in the team. Have you any idea why we might have a psychologist in our team?
ANITA: Well, no, that's what I was saying to the physio, I've had a heart attack not gone mad - I don't need a psychologist!
PSYCHOLOGIST: Ah I see, so you must be wondering what on earth we'd talk about today then!

ANITA: Exactly, yes.
PSYCHOLOGIST: Do you mind if I share a little more about what psychologists do in our team?
ANITA: Yes, ok.
PSYCHOLOGIST: Well having a heart attack can be a really life changing thing – it can affect the way we see ourselves, affect our relationships. We can be troubled by thinking back to the heart attack and our experiences in hospital or have ongoing symptoms that get in the way of us doing things that are important to us. Heart attacks can also be a sign that some of our health habits need to be tweaked. All these things are difficult, and at times we can feel down, frustrated or angry, or scared about the future.
ANITA: Well that's true enough.
PSYCHOLOGIST: We have a Health Psychologist because all those are totally normal things to feel. The Health Psychologist's role is to help people get their head around their heart attack and come up with ideas and strategies to cope and manage to live life in the way they want to going forward. Does that make any sense?
ANITA: Yes, yes it does. It really affected me actually, the heart attack and then the operation and everything ... [continues from there].

Studies suggest that empathy, warmth and the therapeutic relationship are stronger predictors of client outcome than the specific techniques used within psychotherapeutic interventions (Lambert & Barley, 2001). There are various approaches that Health Psychologists may draw on in engaging clients. Each uses a different language and emphasises different approaches that are considered important in assessment and initial engagement with clients. Several stem from counselling approaches and the need to treat clients with unconditional positive regard (Rogers, 1957). In CBT terms the skills from the Cognitive Therapy Rating Scale (James et al., 2001) such as 'agenda setting' and 'collaboration' are used to engage clients from the beginning of an assessment. The approach of Motivational Interviewing discusses the processes of 'engaging' and 'focussing', and emphasises the skills of asking open questions, affirmations, reflective listening and summarising (OARS) throughout motivational interviewing conversations. These, along with agenda setting techniques, help psychologists to build rapport and engage in helpful conversations directed at important issues for the client (Miller & Rollnick, 2012). Health Psychologists may wish to draw on the core features of trauma-informed care in engaging all clients in assessments (trust, choice, empowerment, collaboration and safety, e.g. NHS Education for Scotland, 2020).

In terms of structure, there is a 'funnel' approach to the Health Psychology assessment, moving from the broad open questions ('So can you tell me what brings you here today?' 'How are you getting on with your heart condition just now?') to more specific clarifying questions ('Can I check who is living with you at home?'). It is important to pay attention to the environment of the interview, making sure that as far as possible this is a confidential, safe, comfortable place to talk. The 'classic' clinical interview room is usually a quiet, private room in a healthcare clinic, but Health Psychology assessments may take place at the hospital bedside or ward day room, in clients' own homes or in many other settings, including remotely. During the covid-19 pandemic, Health Psychologists have worked to maintain service provision by conducting assessments remotely, via video call or telephone (Bull, 2020). The recently-developed BPS guidance on working remotely advises psychologists conduct a full risk assessment to explore the client's access to digital technology, privacy of the location and technology used for assessments and how confidentiality will be maintained (British Psychological Society, 2020a, 2020b).

Above all, it is important that the client feels heard, understood and not judged during the assessment process, linking again to Roger's core conditions (Rogers, 1957). A positive experience ensures the psychology 'door' remains open for them in the future, even if the client decides a psychological intervention is not needed at this time, or if the clinical interview is planned as a stand-alone occasion (e.g. psychological screening prior to a medical procedure).

Clinical interview structure and content

The structure of a clinical interview would usually of course start with an *introduction*, which would include introductions to the psychologist, the service and their role. As discussed, this includes checking out and helping to set the person's expectations, agreeing purpose and duration and discussing confidentiality and limits of confidentiality.

Then, within the main part of the biopsychosocial assessment, the most common topic areas for a clinical interview with an adult within either a primary prevention or physical health service might include:

- **Understanding the biological**: where relevant, understanding a person's symptoms, their pathway and journey through the health and social care system in a 'potted summary' of their medical history, medical treatments they are currently and previously received, medications and side effects, investigations or treatments they are waiting or hoping for, physical symptoms they are experiencing in different parts of the body (frequency, intensity, duration), any other treatments

they may be taking to try to improve their condition (e.g. complementary medicines, alcohol, illegal substances).
- **Understanding the psychological**: Understanding in broad terms the reason the person has sought your help, their goals and expectations, their daily routine and health-related behaviours (e.g. current exercise levels, their sleep, impact of their condition, alcohol or smoking). Within a primary prevention service, the focus may be on exploring perceptions of why they are considering making a change, their previous experiences of these and previous barriers and facilitators. Within a physical health service, it would be important to explore the client's own understanding of any health condition(s) and what they think is causing symptoms they are experiencing as well as other illness perceptions such as their view of the timeline (chronicity) and whether they expect to find a cure for their condition. Asking about aspects of life which have changed as a result of their condition including how they see themselves and about distress associated with their condition. Exploring difficult health-related experiences, such as intensive care admissions, traumatic injuries or medical events. Exploring any previous visits to a psychological professional and any mental health history, as well as if they are troubled by any issues from the past (see following section on risk assessment and safeguarding). Asking about thoughts of self-harm, suicidality or risk to others and what may be contributing to or maintaining difficult experiences. Exploring their current coping mechanisms (surrounding their condition or difficult life circumstances and associated distress), including those that may help in the short-term and have some unintended effects. This includes exploring their motivation and confidence/self-efficacy to make some changes to their health-related behaviours or self-management strategies.
- **Understanding the social and environmental**: Understanding where the person lives and with whom, who is important in their life, elements of religion/spirituality, work, and ongoing stressors and inequality issues such as financial instability, ongoing litigation or housing, family or school issues (King's Fund, 2015). Understanding experiences of stigma, prejudice or discrimination, including because of any health conditions. Exploring experiences (good and not so good) with healthcare professionals, to help understand iatrogenic distress. Exploring perceptions of current social support or social isolation, as an important influence on health outcomes but also psychological intervention treatment success. Protective social factors (e.g. family, friends, children, community participation and other meaningful social connections).

The last section of an assessment would usually be a *closing section* where the psychologist and client would summarise what they have learned about the client's pattern of difficulties (beginnings of formulation). It may be useful to provide some introductory psychoeducation (sharing relevant information about psychology), such as surrounding how the biological stress system impacts pain or blood glucose levels, or an introduction to the panic cycle. The closing section should agree a way forward with goals to work together or next steps. This might include discussing with others: the person may wish to discuss with friends or family before deciding on a treatment option. Equally the psychologist may offer the client a further assessment session and/or to discuss formulation and treatment planning with colleagues or options for an onward referral to another service.

Our experience of Health Psychology in clinical practice

In our experience, often services have their own preferred assessment template or topic guide with suggested questions exploring these areas. However, we tend to find we spend more time than our colleagues from other psychological professions exploring a client's health beliefs and experiences within the healthcare system. These can be vital in guiding our Health Psychology formulation and also in assessing suitability for clinical Health Psychology services. In most cases, such services are funded to help clients who are experiencing self-management difficulties and psychological distress relating to one or more physical health conditions (see formulation chapter) and aim ultimately to improve their long-term condition management and health outcomes as well as psychological wellbeing.

In this assessment extract example (Box 8.3), the psychologist asks questions to explore the physical symptoms Anita has mentioned when beginning her prescribed exercises following her heart attack. The psychologist's questions in this example aim to empathically establish the timeline, symptoms experienced, and Anita's beliefs about what is causing her physical symptoms in this assessment.

Box 8.3 Exploring health symptoms and beliefs

PSYCHOLOGIST: So, Anita you've been telling me there about some really scary sensations you're getting whenever you start to exercise now, like at the rehab class. Did you ever have these physical symptoms before the heart attack?

ANITA: Not at all, it's only now after my stent, when I start to do my exercises I can feel my heart beating so hard and fast, like it's trying to get out of my chest, I feel so hot and faint and I get a dry mouth feeling just like before the heart attack.

> PSYCHOLOGIST: So, what do you think is going on there, inside you?
> ANITA: I think it must be my body saying 'woah there, stop that exercise right now, or else you'll have another heart attack'. Like a warning sign that you don't want to work the arteries too hard or the stent will collapse. When I get them, I just go into panic mode, and I start to think of myself ending up on the operating table again like when I had the heart attack.
> PSYCHOLOGIST: I see that sounds horrible, and what do you do then?
> ANITA: I stop what I'm doing and go and sit down or lie down until it all calms down.
> PSYCHOLOGIST: And how long does that tend to take, do you think?
> ANITA: Probably about 15 or 20 minutes or so, though I feel shaky for a bit afterwards.
> PSYCHOLOGIST: Wow that sounds a difficult experience, I think I have an idea of what may be going on there, if I could share with you?

In this example, the exploration of Anita's experiences and health beliefs, along with previous conversations with Anita's cardiologist and physiotherapist (who have confirmed that exercise is medically safe for Anita) helps the psychologist formulate that Anita's current physical symptoms are driven by panic rather than a recurrence of her heart attack. The psychologist can go on to providing some basic psychoeducation about panic in the next section of the interview and then move on to collaborative formulation and treatment planning.

Standardised psychological and behavioural measures

There are a range of psychometrically validated measures typically used in conjunction with a clinical interview in clinical Health Psychology services. Some are generically used in health services, for example the Hospital Anxiety and Depression Scale (Zigmond & Snaith, 1983) designed for hospital populations, others are part of the core data set within primary mental healthcare services, such as Patient Health Questionnaire-9 (Kroenke et al., 2001), Generalised Anxiety Disorder-7 (Spitzer et al., 2006), CORE-10 (Barkham et al., 2013), others are health condition specific, such as the Diabetes Distress Scale (Polonsky et al., 2005) and Pain Anxiety Symptoms Scale (McCracken et al., 1992). When setting up new service we sometimes have the freedom to choose standardised measures for service evaluation. Health Psychologists may wish to make decisions based on what might be collected in other parts of a service, what is specific to the population (e.g.

Pain Self-Efficacy Questionnaire: Nicholas, 2007) and so clinically useful, what might be the main measures in the research field if considering writing up a service evaluation for publication. It is important to think also of the frequency that these are needed (e.g. first and last session, or weekly), format (could this be completed quickly on a tablet or emailed via Microsoft forms, depending on copyright restrictions), response burden with impacts on therapeutic engagement and how to be sensitive to (often hidden) literacy issues or language completion issues. In Box 8.4, we include some of the Health Psychology areas where standardised measures have been developed, we recommend readers to Benyamini et al. (2015) for a hugely comprehensive overview of these. Psychologists will of course wish to undertake personal study, undertake practice and feedback and any other training recommended in test manuals in order to reach competence to deliver assessment measures. The BPS (British Psychological Society, 2020b) also suggest that where a standardised assessment measure is delivered remotely, psychologists should consider how to deliver this consistently with its intended construct validity and following the conditions stated in any test manual.

> **Box 8.4. Broad areas of measurement relevant to Health Psychology, including examples of specific measurement tools**
>
> - **Anxiety and depression symptoms**: Hospital Anxiety and Depression Scale (HADS) (Zigmond & Snaith, 1983), Centre for Epidemiological Studies of Depression questionnaire (CES-D) (Radloff, 1977), Generalised Anxiety Disorder-7 questionnaire (GAD-7) (Spitzer et al. 2006).
> - **Coping**: Brief COPE (Carver, 1997).
> - **Health behaviour**: including self-report measures, e.g. International Physical Activity Questionnaire – Short Form (IPAQ-SF; Lee et al., 2011), and pedometers.
> - **Illness representations**: Revised Illness Perceptions Questionnaire (IPQ-R) (Moss-Morris et al., 2002).
> - **Medication adherence**: electronic caps for pill bottles, and medication adherence beliefs e.g. Eight-Item Morisky Medication Adherence Scale (MMAS-8; Morisky et al., 2008).
> - **Neuropsychological assessment**: Mini Mental Status Examination (Folstein et al., 1975)
> - **Pain-related distress**: Pain Anxiety Symptoms Scale (PASS) (McCracken et al., 1992).

- **Post-traumatic stress symptoms**: The Impact of Events Scale – Revised (IES-R) (Weiss & Marmar, 1997).
- **Psychological adjustment**: Patient Health Questionnaire-9 (Kroenke et al., 2001), Satisfaction with Life Scale (Diener et al., 1985).
- **Quality of life**: MOS 36-item Short-Form Health Survey (SF-36) (Ware & Sherbourne, 1992).
- **Self-rated health**: single item measures (e.g. Jürges et al., 2008).
- **Social cognitions**: including intentions, self-efficacy and norms measured through Likert scales (e.g. Conner & Sparks, 2005).
- **Social support**: Social Provisions Scale (Cutrona & Russell, 1987).
- **Stress**: Perceived Stress Scale (Cohen et al., 1983).

Whether clients complete these on entry to the service, immediately before or during assessment, it is important to fully explain their purpose and reflect together on the impressions they are offering. In the example below (Box 8.5), this is shared with Anita towards the end of the clinical interview, to add to the beginning of formulation.

Box 8.5 Discussing information from within standardised measures

PSYCHOLOGIST: I wanted to say thank you, Anita, for filling in those service questionnaires for us before coming along today. They can help add to our ideas of what's been troubling you and also can help us evaluate the service, to see if things change for you over time. How did you find completing them?
ANITA: Yes, they were ok, they didn't take very long once I got going.
PSYCHOLOGIST: Good to hear, would you mind if I share some information about them?
ANITA: Yes, please do.
PSYCHOLOGIST: Well this one here, the Hospital Anxiety and Depression Scale, asks about possible symptoms of stress or anxiety and also low mood or depression for people with health conditions. If we add up the boxes you've ticked there, it would suggest you're experiencing clinical levels of anxiety with a score of 16 out of 21, but not depression with a score of 4. What do you make of that?
ANITA: Well, yes, it's like we've been talking about, that sudden feeling of panic, but no I don't think I'm depressed.

> PSYCHOLOGIST: Absolutely, yes, and that feeling of being tense all the time that you mentioned. So that fits for you. I hope that after working together, if you do that questionnaire for us again, we'll see that score reducing. Is there anything else you wanted to add or ask about that part of our assessment before we move onto thinking about your goals for our work together?

Here the psychologist asks permission from Anita to discuss the findings of pre-assessment HADS questionnaire (Zigmond & Snaith, 1983) and checks out her beliefs and understandings, using the elicit–provide–elicit framework from motivational interviewing (Miller & Rollnick, 2012). This helps the psychologist to share the service's focus on monitoring and quality improvement and orient the client towards the final part of the clinical interview. The elicit–provide–elicit approach may also be useful in sharing other medical information to add to the assessment ('I wonder if we could look together at your recent scan results to see if we can make sense of this?').

Risk assessment and safeguarding

As part of a Health Psychologist's duty of care and responsibilities (Health and Care Professions Council, 2015), Health Psychology assessments must also consider a client's risk of harm to themselves or other people. The Department of Health and Social Care's Best Practice in Managing Risk (Department of Health and Social Care, 2009) views risk as a judgement relating to the likelihood, imminence and severity of a negative event occurring, including self-harm, self-neglect or neglect of dependents, and/or a worsening of their health condition leading to a medical emergency. These are unfortunately very relevant to consider in those we commonly see in clinical practice. Living with a long-term health condition is a key risk factor for suicidal thoughts and behaviours (Franklin et al., 2017). Living with a physical health condition can be life-limiting, extremely stressful and frustrating with the demands of treatment and medical appointments gruelling and relentless. Where an adult or child's health is worsening and they are not able to self-manage their condition there may be safeguarding concerns for the vulnerable adult or children or others they usually care for. Unfortunately, research suggests complex relationships between poverty, adverse childhood experiences (ACEs), experiences of domestic violence and other social inequalities and the risk of developing some long-term conditions (e.g. Steel et al., 2014; Chandan et al., 2019; Scottish Government, 2020). This means that psychologists working in this area need to be able to identify and respond appropriately to risk and safeguarding concerns.

When assessing risk, the National Institute for Health and Care Excellence guidelines on the long-term management of self-harm state that risk assessment tools and scales should not be used to predict suicide or self-harm or to decide on treatment approaches (National Institute for Health and Care Excellence, 2011). A recent review of the evidence also agreed that no individual risk prediction instrument offers sufficient sensitivity and specificity to inform clinically useful decision-making (Zortea et al. 2020). A national inquiry into the topic (National Confidential Inquiry into Suicide and Safety in Mental Health, 2018) concluded that on their own, tools and scales have little place in preventing suicide. Instead, management of risk needs to be personalised and individualised with a collaborative approach, ensuring 'good information gathered surrounding (i) the current situation, (ii) history or risk and (iii) social factors' (p. 20) including input from family and friends where possible. A formulation tool, such as 5Ps (Kuyken et al., 2009; see also Chapter 9, this volume) might be useful in bringing together information about risk to help inform decisions about helping prevent harm. Often professionals can feel unskilled to raise and discuss such issues or respond to disclosures such as of current or past abuse. Attending local suicide awareness and safeguarding training is a vital first step in this regard. In our experience, routinely asking a simple question during assessments such as 'do you ever have really difficult thoughts about yourself and your situation?' can help the person feel validated to discuss suicidal ideation and other risks. At times, direct questions may be needed to assess risk. However, clients may make a disclosure at any time during treatment and may be more likely to do so later on in treatment when trust is built than at a first assessment session. Therefore, it is vitally important to be ready for this and also sensitive to exploring cues from a client (e.g. mention of problems with a partner or children, an uncharacteristically dishevelled appearance, or mention of being 'fed up with it all', or reaching 'the end of their tether').

Poor reactions to disclosures by psychologists who may lack confidence ('oh goodness well I'm not the right person to talk to about this') or react in a non-collaborative manner ('you've mentioned feeling really down at times so I must immediately tell the service manager and your GP') can cause a therapeutic rupture. This can lead to a client experiencing shame and being less likely to disclose this in future or seek help for their difficulty. It is important to remember that while all disclosures should be taken seriously, thoughts of wanting to escape from a relentless long-term condition are understandably relatively common. Many complex factors influence whether suicidal ideation becomes suicidal behaviour (O'Connor & Kirtley, 2018). Again, we would consider attending training on how to conduct brief suicide and safeguarding assessments is essential to build skills and confidence. Generally, these suggest first thanking the person for their disclosure and providing empathy ('Thank you for telling me about this important issue for you, I'm sorry that you're feeling like this') before asking permission to explore the issue further ('I know we had planned X but this feels important, could we spend time now talking more about this so I can get the whole picture?') and sensitively listening.

The service and organisation's policies on safeguarding, risk and personal security should detail the remit of the psychologist's service and the appropriate organisational resources and services that need to be involved in different scenarios. Applying our Health Psychology theory, it can be useful to formulate these into if-then plans (e.g. Gollwitzer, 1999) on what to do if key scenarios were to arise, with telephone numbers of support agencies included. This will help the psychologist sensitively listen, assess risk and guide to collaboratively agreeing next steps with the client to enable them to link in with specialist services or the other members of the team depending on the risk issue identified. It is vital to collaboratively agree with the client who will be informed of the conversation and how (e.g. the GP as the coordinator of the care via letter, or the person's medical consultant), such as:

> It's been really useful for me to get a better idea of these upsetting thoughts you've been having and to make some plans on how to keep you safe if the difficult feelings and urges return. Now perhaps we could decide who in your medical team might need to know about our plans?

The discussion of confidentiality and the limits of confidentiality held at the beginning of the assessment will very much help with this. All practising psychologists should undertake regular consultation or supervision (British Psychological Society, 2017) to ensure their safe and effective practice in clinical settings, in which it would be useful to discuss and reflect on cases where risk could be a factor.

Conclusion

In this chapter we have aimed to present a practical overview of assessment in Health Psychology clinical practice, including presenting a biopsychosocial approach to assessment, considering how to integrate self-report questionnaire measures and considering risk and safeguarding. This is based on our own practice in a range of primary prevention and physical health settings, but is by no means the only approach. We would be very glad to continue discussing with other psychologists working in these areas to learn and share ideas for engaging and collaborative Health Psychology assessments. Given that formulation is the sense-making of assessment, these two are inextricably linked. Our formulation chapter, which follows, presents practical approaches to formulating clients' problems in Health Psychology clinical practice.

References

Barkham, M., Bewick, B., Mullin, T., Gilbody, S., Connell, J., Cahill, J., ... & Evans, C. (2013). The CORE-10: A short measure of psychological distress for routine use in the psychological therapies. *Counselling and Psychotherapy Research*, 13(1), 3–13.
Benyamini, Y., Johnston, M., & Karademas, E. C. (eds). (2015). *Assessment in Health Psychology* (vol. 2). Göttingen: Hogrefe Publishing.
British Psychological Society. (2015). *Qualification in Health Psychology (Stage 2) candidate handbook*. Leicester: British Psychological Society.
British Psychological Society. (2017). *British Psychological Society practice guidelines*, 3rd edition. Leicester: British Psychological Society. Retrieved from www.bps.org.uk/sites/bps.org.uk/files/Policy/Policy%20-%20Files/BPS%20Practice%20Guidelines%20(Third%20Edition).pdf
British Psychological Society. (2020a). *Adaptations to psychological practice: Continuing guidance during COVID-19 pandemic*. Leicester: British Psychological Society. Retrieved from www.bps.org.uk/sites/www.bps.org.uk/files/Policy/Policy%20-20Files/Adaptations%20to%20psychological%20practice%20-%20interim%20guidance%20during%20Covid-19.pdf.
British Psychological Society. (2020b). Psychological assessment undertaken remotely. Retrieved from www.bps.org.uk/sites/www.bps.org.uk/files/Policy/Policy%20-%20Files/Psychological%20assessment%20undertaken%20remotely.pdf.
Bull, E. R., Hart, J. K., Swift, J., Baxter, K., McLauchlan, N., Joseph, S., & Byrne-Davis, L. M. (2019). An organisational participatory research study of the feasibility of the behaviour change wheel to support clinical teams implementing new models of care. *BMC Health Services Research*, 19(1), 1–12.
Bull, E. R. (2020). Reflecting on the 'corona coaster': The impact on Health Psychology interventions (based on DHP 'Celebrating Health Psychology' webinar talk New Ways of Working in Practice). *Health Psychology Update*, 29, 24–25.
Carver, C. S. (1997). You want to measure coping but your protocol's too long: Consider the Brief COPE. *International Journal of Behavioral Medicine*, 4, 92–100.
Chandan, J. S., Thomas, T., Raza, K., Bradbury-Jones, C., Taylor, J., Bandyopadhyay, S., & Nirantharakumar, K. (2019). Intimate partner violence and the risk of developing fibromyalgia and chronic fatigue syndrome. *Journal of Interpersonal Violence* (online ahead of print). doi:10.1177/0886260519888515
Cohen, S., Kamarck, T., & Mermelstein, R. (1983). Perceived stress scale (PSS). *Journal of Health and Social Behaviour*, 24, 385–396.
Conner, M., & Sparks, P. (2005). The theory of planned behaviour and health behaviours. In M. Conner & P. Norman (eds), *Predicting health behaviour* (pp. 170–222). Maidenhead: McGraw-Hill Education.

Cutrona, C. E., & Russell, D. W. (1987). The provisions of social relationships and adaptations to stress. In W. H. Jones & D. Perlman (eds), *Advances in personal relationships*, vol. 1, pp. 37–67. Greenwich, CT: JAI Press.

Debono, D., Taylor, N., Lipworth, W., Greenfield, D., Travaglia, J., Black, D., & Braithwaite, J. (2017). Applying the theoretical domains framework to identify barriers and targeted interventions to enhance nurses' use of electronic medication management systems in two Australian hospitals. *Implementation Science*, 12(1), 1–13.

Department of Health and Social Care. (2009). *Best practice in managing risk: Principles and evidence for best practice in the assessment and management of risk to self and others in mental health services*. London: Department of Health and Social Care.

Diener, E. D., Emmons, R. A., Larsen, R. J., & Griffin, S. (1985). The Satisfaction with Life Scale. *Journal of Personality Assessment*, 49(1), 71–75.

Folstein, M. F., Folstein, S. E., & McHugh, P. R. (1975). 'Mini-mental state': A practical method for grading the cognitive state of patients for the clinician. *Journal of Psychiatric Research*, 12(3), 189–198.

Franklin, J. C., Ribeiro, J. D., Fox, K. R., Bentley, K. H., Kleiman, E. M., Huang, X., ... & Nock, M. K. (2017). Risk factors for suicidal thoughts and behaviors: A meta-analysis of 50 years of research. *Psychological Bulletin*, 143(2), 187.

Gollwitzer, P. M. (1999). Implementation intentions: Strong effects of simple plans. *American Psychologist*, 54(7), 493.

Health and Care Professions Council. (2015). *Standards of proficiency: Practitioner psychologists*. London: Health and Care Professions Council.

Hussain, H., & Knowles, N. (2020). *Applying behavioural science principles to the work of Bradford's Young COVID Ambassadors*. Bradford: Bradford Youth Service. Retrieved from www.local.gov.uk/sites/default/files/documents/Nicky%20Knowles%20and%20Hannah%20Hussain%2C%20Bradford%20Council.pdf.

James, I. A., Blackburn, I. M., & Reichelt, F. K. (2001). Manual of the revised cognitive therapy scale. Unpublished manuscript, Newcastle Cognitive and Behavioural Therapies Centre, Newcastle, UK.

Johnston, M. (1994). Health Psychology: Current trends. *The Psychologist*, 7, 114–118.

Johnstone, L., & Dallos, R. (2013). *Formulation in psychology and psychotherapy: Making sense of people's problems*. Abingdon: Routledge.

Jürges, H., Avendano, M., & Mackenbach, J. P. (2008). Are different measures of self-rated health comparable? An assessment in five European countries. *European Journal of Epidemiology*, 23(12), 773–781.

King's Fund. (2015). *Intentional whole health system redesign Southcentral Foundation's 'Nuka' system of care*. London: King's Fund.

Kroenke, K., Spitzer, R. L., & Williams, J. B. (2001). The PHQ-9: validity of a brief depression severity measure. *Journal of General Internal Medicine*, 16(9), 606–613.

Kuyken, W., Padesky, C.A. & Dudley, R. (2009). *Collaborative Case Conceptualization*. New York: Guilford Press.

Lambert, M. J., & Barley, D. E. (2001). Research summary on the therapeutic relationship and psychotherapy outcome. *Psychotherapy: Theory, Research, Practice, Training*, 38(4), 357–361. doi:10.1037/0033-3204.38.4.357.

Lee, P.H., Macfarlane, D.J., Lam, T.H., Stewart, S.M. (2011). Validity of the international physical activity questionnaire short form (IPAQ-SF): A systematic review. *International Journal of Behavioral Nutrition and Physical Activity*, 8, 115.

McCracken, L. M., Zayfert, C., & Gross, R. T. (1992). The Pain Anxiety Symptoms Scale: development and validation of a scale to measure fear of pain. *Pain*, 50(1), 67–73.

Miller, W. R., & Rollnick, S. (2012). *Motivational interviewing: Helping people change*. New York: Guilford Press.

Monaghan, M., Singh, C., Streisand, R., & Cogen, F. R. (2010). Screening and identification of children and adolescents at risk for depression during a diabetes clinic visit. *Diabetes Spectrum*, 23(1), 25–31.

Morisky D. E., Ang A., Krousel-Wood M., Ward H. J. (2008) Predictive validity of a medication adherence measure in an outpatient setting. *Journal of Clinical Hypertension*, 10(5), 348–354. doi:10.1111/j.1751-7176.2008.07572.x.

Moss-Morris, R. (2013). Adjusting to chronic illness: Time for a unified theory. *British Journal of Health Psychology*, 18, 681–686.

Moss-Morris, R., Weinman, J., Petrie, K., Horne, R., Cameron, L., Buick, D., et al. (2002). The revised Illness Perception Questionnaire (IPQ-R). *Psychology and Health*, 17, 1–16.

Mullings, L., & Schulz, A. J. (2006). Intersectionality and Health: An Introduction. In A. J. Schulz & L. Mullings (eds), *Gender, race, class, & health: Intersectional approaches*, pp. 3–17. New York: Jossey-Bass/Wiley.

National Confidential Inquiry into Suicide and Safety in Mental Health. (2018). *The assessment of clinical risk in mental health services*. Manchester: The University of Manchester.

National Institute for Health and Care Excellence. (2011). *Self-harm in over 8s: Long-term management*. Clinical Guideline 133. London: NICE.

NHS Education for Scotland. (2020). Transforming psychological trauma: National Trauma Training Programme online resources. Retrieved fromhttps://transformingpsychologicaltrauma.scot/media/w3hpiif4/nes-national-trauma-training-programme-training-resources.pdf (accessed 24 March 2021).

Nicholas, M. K. (2007). The pain self-efficacy questionnaire: taking pain into account. *European Journal of Pain*, 11(2), 153–163.

Nueberger, J., and Tallis, R. (1999). Education and debate. Do we need a new word for patients? Let's do away with 'patients' Commentary: Leave well alone. *BMJ*, 318(7200), 1756–1758.

O'Connor RC, Kirtley OJ. (2018) The integrated motivational-volitional model of suicidal behaviour. *Philosophical Transactions of the Royal Society B*, 373, 20170268.

Parry, S. (ed). (2019) *The handbook of brief therapies: A practical guide*. Thousand Oaks, CA: Sage Publishing.

Pickersgill, M. (2020). Uncertainty work as ontological negotiation: adjudicating access to therapy in clinical psychology. *Sociology of Health & Illness*, 42, 84–98.

Polonsky, W. H., Fisher, L., Earles, J., Dudl, R. J., Lees, J., Mullan, J., & Jackson, R. A. (2005). Assessing psychosocial distress in diabetes: development of the diabetes distress scale. *Diabetes Care*, 28(3), 626–631.

Psychological Professions Network. (2020). Maximising the impact of psychological practice in physical healthcare: Discussion paper. Retrieved fromwww.ppn.nhs. uk/resources/ppn-publications/34-maximising-the-impact-of-psychological-practice-in-physical-healthcare-discussion-paper/fil (accessed 24 March 2021).

Radloff, L. S. (1977). The CES-D scale: a self-report depression scale for research in the general population. *Applied Psychological Measures*, 1, 385–401.

Roth, A. D. & Pilling, S. (2016). *A competence framework for psychological interventions with people with persistent physical health problems*. London: University College London. Retrieved fromwww.ucl.ac.uk/pals/sites/pals/files/migrated-files/Physical_Core_competences.pdf.

Refsgaard, B., & Frederiksen, K. (2013). Illness-related emotional experiences of patients living with incurable lung cancer: A qualitative metasynthesis. *Cancer Nursing*, 36(3), 221–228.

Rogers, C. (1957). The necessary and sufficient conditions of therapeutic personality change. *Journal of Consulting Psychology*. 21(2): 95–103.

Scottish Government. (2020). *Adverse Childhood Experiences (ACEs) and Trauma*. Edinburgh: Scottish Government.

Spitzer, R. L., Kroenke, K., Williams, J. B., & Löwe, B. (2006). A brief measure for assessing generalized anxiety disorder: the GAD-7. *Archives of Internal Medicine*, 166(10), 1092–1097.

Stam. H. J. (2015). A critical history of Health Psychology and its relationship to biomedicine. In M. Murray (ed.), *Critical Health Psychology*, pp. 19–35. Basingstoke: Macmillan International Higher Education.

Steel, N., Hardcastle, A. C., Bachmann, M. O., Richards, S. H., Mounce, L. T. A., Clark, A., ... & Campbell, J. (2014). Economic inequalities in burden of illness, diagnosis and treatment of five long-term conditions in England: panel study. *BMJ Open*, 4(10).

Townend, M., and Grant, A. (2017). Assessment in CBT: The ideographic approach. In A. Grant, M. Townend, J. Mills & A. Cockx (eds), *Assessment and case formulation in cognitive behavioural therapy*. Thousand Oaks, CA: Sage Publishing.

Ware, J. E., & Sherbourne, C. D. (1992). The MOS 36-item short-form health survey (SF-36): I. Conceptual framework and item selection. *Medical Care*, 30, 473–483.

Watson, J. (ed.) (2019). *Drop the Disorder! Challenging the culture of psychiatric diagnosis*. Monmouth: PCCS Books.

Weiss, D. S., & Marmar, C. R. (1997). The impact of event scale – revised. In: J. P. Wilson & T. M. Keane (eds), *Assessing psychological trauma and PTSD*, pp. 399–411. New York: Guilford Press.

Zigmond, A. S., & Snaith, R. P. (1983). The hospital anxiety and depression scale. *Acta psychiatrica scandinavica*, 67(6), 361–370.

Zortea, T. C., Cleare, S. Melson, A. J., Wetherall, K., & O'Connor, R. C. (2020). Understanding and managing suicide risk. *British Medical Bulletin*, 134(1), 73–84.

9 Formulation in Health Psychology clinical practice

Hannah Dale and Eleanor Bull

Introduction

Assessment and formulation are two sides of the same coin; formulation is the sense making of our assessment information which helps tailor an intervention accordingly. Like assessment (see previous chapter), formulation (sometimes called case conceptualisation) is a core psychological intervention competency, taught to doctoral level and a key area of Health Psychologists' competence (British Psychological Society, 2015; Health and Care Professions Council, 2015; Roth & Pilling, 2016). The history of formulation in psychology is well described elsewhere (British Psychological Society, 2011; Johnstone & Dallos, 2013). In brief, psychological formulation formally emerged in the 1950s and has increasingly become part of psychology practice (British Psychological Society, 2011).

Formulation has a variety of different definitions but broadly involves summarising the client's core difficulties in a systematic way, relating factors to one another and drawing on psychological theories and principles (Johnstone & Dallos, 2013). According to one all-encompassing definition,

> a formulation is the tool used by clinicians to relate theory to practice. Clinicians use theoretical as well as practical knowledge to guide their thinking about the problems and difficulties presented by the people who come to them for help, and this combination of ideas helps them decide how best to help those people.
>
> (Butler, 1998, p. 2)

This is usually a shared and ongoing process during therapy as new information comes to light and the psychologist and client work together to integrate this. Formulation skills are an essential part of Health Psychology and can be used directly with clients and more indirectly, such as working with multi-disciplinary colleagues to try to help them make sense of the

DOI: 10.4324/9781003120469-10

difficulties a particular client is experiencing and to work in a psychologically-informed way. This work requires the Health Psychologist to gather, make sense of and communicate sensitively about a wide range of sometimes conflicting information taking a truly biopsychosocial approach (Engel, 1980). Formulation approaches can differ in terms of the factors that are seen as most relevant, the psychological concepts drawn upon, the emphasis placed on the extent of 'truth' of the formulation, the way formulation is used in therapy, and how much the approach adopts an expert versus collaborative stance (Johnstone & Dallos, 2013). Psychologists often integrate different models of formulation as this can serve to provide a broader perspective than one alone (British Psychological Society, 2011).

In this chapter, we build on the work discussed in the previous chapter on assessment by discussing how we can make sense of information gathered from clients with the help of several different formulation approaches. This includes tools we have developed and used in our clinical practice based on various theory-based approaches including the behaviour change wheel (Michie et al., 2014), theoretical domains framework (TDF; Cane et al., 2012) and the motivation, action, prompts model (Dixon and Johnston, 2020a, 2020b). Some of these approaches are more commonly applied in Health Psychology at a population or community level, but we find them equally applicable to individual level formulation. We consider how multiple formulation tools may help us look with 'different lenses' on the same problem, enabling a full understanding to best help our clients. We use several case examples covering a range of difficulties to illustrate the strategies and key considerations. We also provide a table (Table 9.2) in which we rate each tool on key characteristics, based on our own experiences working with them in clinical practice. These include our view of their generalisability to different problems, their comprehensiveness in using relevant theory within primary prevention/physical health services, how strongly the formulation is linked to interventions strategies and their accessibility for shared formulation with clients. We hope this pragmatic tool can help Health Psychologists to choose a useful tool(s) to best fit a particular client or service. Finally, we discuss the types of interventions Health Psychologists may deliver based on assessment and formulation, including presenting a stepped care model.

As we stated in our previous chapter, there are many different terms for Health Psychology clinical services and the people they serve. In this chapter we refer to services to help healthy people keep well as 'primary prevention services' and services to help people adjust to, cope and manage acute or long-term conditions as 'physical health services' (sometimes these are referred to as Clinical Health Psychology services). We refer to 'clients' rather than 'patients', even though the latter is still a commonly used term in healthcare. While the term client could be suggestive of a 'purchaser-provider' relationship

(Nueberger & Tallis, 1999) we feel it helps to describe people playing an active role in their treatment and denotes a collaborative relationship which is vital in the work Health Psychologists do to help empower people.

Formulation in our roles as Health Psychologists

Just as theory-based population interventions are more effective than those without a theoretical basis (Craig et al., 2008), developing one-to-one interventions based on formulation is considered vital to effective treatment (Johnstone & Dallos, 2013). This is especially when working at higher levels of intensity where interventions are fully tailored to each individual (Dixon and Johnston, 2010; Health Education England, 2021) However, some authors have suggested that formulation in clinical Health Psychology is not well defined (Hilton & Johnston, 2017). We have enjoyed using formulation as Health Psychologists in a range of clinical practice settings, from primary care, diabetes and pain services to hepatitis, oncology, substance misuse and sexual health and blood borne virus services. In our roles we also have the privilege of helping upskill others in using formulation, including Stage 1 and 2 trainee and junior Health Psychologists and multidisciplinary colleagues. As with our assessment work, our brilliant psychology and multidisciplinary teams and colleagues have helped us shape our ideas about what formulation approaches may be common to most psychological professions and where our field tends to add expertise. We find it useful to have a visual representation of formulations and to share and learn from case examples, so in this chapter we include several worked examples from three fictional case vignettes summarised in Boxes 9.1, 9.2 and 9.3. Further information about each case is added within the formulation examples.

> **Box 9.1 Case vignette: Anita**
>
> Anita is a 61-year-old lady who had a myocardial infarction (heart attack) four months ago. She was treated with coronary angioplasty (with a metal mesh stent to widen her coronary artery). She was referred to the Health Psychology cardiac service by one of the team physiotherapists who said she was not engaging well in her rehabilitation programme as although she attended appointments, she appeared anxious and fear-avoidant. Anita has tried exercising but as soon as she does, she gets a pain in her chest, becomes very anxious and stops. After about 10–15 minutes, the pain subsides. While not sure at first about seeing a psychologist, Anita then said she would like help coping with her heart attack, especially with the fear that it's going to come back at any time.

Box 9.2 Case vignette: John

John is a 54-year-old man who lives with his wife and 18-year-old son. He works in IT and generally works over 40 hours per week. John was diagnosed with type 2 diabetes last year and has a body mass index (BMI) of 36. Otherwise, John feels well and has no other physical or mental health conditions diagnosed, though does have a history of depression. John's GP has noted that he has found it hard to accept his diagnosis of diabetes and although he attends for invited appointments, he fails to monitor his blood sugar levels as advised, and has not made any changes to his diet or exercise. They have referred John for further support to a Health Psychologist. The Health Psychologist and John met twice for a comprehensive assessment involving a clinical interview and standardised measures (e.g. the diabetes distress scale), and a wide range of information was gathered.

Box 9.3 Case vignette: Sinead

Sinead is a 22-year-old medical student who lives at home with her mum and younger brother. Sinead is a high-achieving, hard-working student with an active social life and a part-time bar job. Sinead developed widespread pain and fatigue about two years ago following a winter virus. Following a frustrating number of tests and investigations which drew a blank, Sinead was diagnosed last year by a rheumatologist as having fibromyalgia. Sinead did not react positively to this diagnosis: she had heard from other students that fibromyalgia was not a real condition and people were given this diagnosis if they were lazy and rested too much. As a result, Sinead did not initially want to be referred to her local pain self-management team which includes a Health Psychologist. Instead, she pushed herself harder than ever to maintain her studies, social life and job. Over time, her pain and flare ups increased so much that after a busy week of placement she could end up in bed all weekend and had started to miss bar shifts. With encouragement from her mum who was worried about her, Sinead reluctantly made an appointment with the Health Psychologist for help coping with her pain and fatigue.

Formulation tools in Health Psychology

There are a range of theories, models and approaches to understanding change used within Health Psychology and the therapeutic traditions more broadly that are relevant to the work of Health Psychologists in practice. A formulation is only ever as good as the information feeding into it, so depends on a psychologist conducting a thorough and collaborative assessment (see our previous chapter on assessment). The choice of formulation tool may also influence our assessment structure or questioning. For example, within a sexual health service, if we plan to use the TDF model as a formulation tool, we might purposefully explore a client's beliefs within its different domains in an assessment, such as a person's beliefs about the consequences of not using condoms. However, we would most often use the tools iteratively, gathering information during an initial assessment, using clinical judgement to apply this to a tool, usually sharing and reforming this with the client and continuing to build and evolve the formulation as necessary across the whole therapeutic process.

Below we summarise 10 approaches to formulation. These include a brief summary of the therapeutic approach or tradition, key concepts and a worked case example illustrating the new learning this tool may add to our shared understanding of a client's strengths and difficulties. The first four of these are derived from the 'three waves' of cognitive behavioural therapy (CBT), followed by two models derived from decades of Health Psychology research on adjustment and illness cognitions. The final four tools relate to perhaps the most practice-focussed of our behaviour change theories and approaches, including three developed to help non-psychology specialists use behavioural theories and methods. This is not an exhaustive list; we share those we have found to be most useful within our own practice. As we can only include a summary of each, we strongly urge readers to use the references we have provided or other relevant sources to fully immerse themselves in any unfamiliar models prior to applying them within client-facing work. In this chapter we take a pragmatic view of theories and models using the terms somewhat interchangeably. We use the word 'tool' to mean a visual outline version of the theory/model which a psychologist can use to assist their client work.

Antecedents, behaviours and consequences functional analysis

Understanding behaviours in terms of their antecedents and consequences has a long history in psychology stemming from early learning theories (Johnston, 2016) and often applied as a formulation approach in cognitive behaviour therapy (Kuyken et al., 2009). It aims to understand the functions, drivers, and reinforcing and punishing factors that serve to increase or decrease likelihood of helpful and unhelpful behaviours. In formulation, psychologists and clients explore the events, thoughts, feelings or behaviours leading up to the behaviour (antecedents) and those the client experiences after (consequences). This is usually focused on one or two key behaviours, however multiple antecedents, behaviours and consequences (ABC) analyses may be relevant for one client. Within Health Psychology, this has diverse applications, including exploring binge eating behaviour, alcohol use, non-adherence to medication, sedentary behaviour, pain behaviours and many hundreds of others. Sometimes it can be helpful to explore both the short and long-term consequences of a behaviour, since we can discover that our behaviours often have short-term reinforcement factors (e.g. pleasure from eating chocolate bar) and longer-term punishment factors (e.g. guilt and shame for breaking healthy eating intentions and worry about health or weight gain). Using the case vignette of Anita, Table 9.1 shows how an ABC formulation can be applied. From this, we can see that it is Anita's hypervigilance and pain experienced in her chest, with accompanying thoughts about having a heart attack, that led her to stop exercising. In fact, it is likely to be the physical symptoms of the body's normal anxiety and panic response and normal exercise-related changes causing her heart to beat faster, which she notices with her close monitoring and may interpret as pain. Stopping or not doing exercise is a behaviour that is reinforced since in the short-term her chest pain subsides as she 'escapes' the anxiety-provoking situation. However, in the longer term, she remains unfit, anxious, has low self-efficacy to change, and at increased risk of another coronary event. This analysis doesn't specifically link to intervention approaches, however it would point to utilising psychoeducation through sharing the ABC formulation, using thought challenging exercises and graded goal setting to gradually build up exercise with support from professionals.

Table 9.1 ABC functional analysis example

Antecedent	Behaviour	Consequence(s)
Anxious thoughts about having another heart attack while exercising Closely monitoring body symptoms (hypervigilance) Notices heart beating fast and pain in chest	Stops exercising	Short term: pain in chest goes away Long term: remains unfit, anxious and lacking in confidence and at increased risk of another coronary event

Cognitive behavioural therapy five areas approach

If the original behavioural model drawn on in CBT is the ABC model, most would agree that the original cognitive model is Beck's cognitive theory of depression (e.g. Beck, 1967). Beck and his contemporaries drew attention to the role of biased and unhelpful thinking patterns in maintaining depression and other mood disorders. However, such disorder-specific formulation models are limited in their generalisability to the wide range of problems clients may struggle with and can be difficult to offer as a shared tool with clients (Williams & Garland, 2002). The five areas approach (Williams & Garland, 2002) was developed as a more generic, simple and applicable approach to CBT formulation. This explores five areas of a client's experiences to build a sense of the links between (a) a difficult situation the client is experiencing, (b) a client's thoughts associated with the situation, (c) emotions accompanying difficult thoughts, (d) bodily changes which may arise from such thoughts and feelings, and (e) their behaviour, including what they do and don't do as a result. It is important to then discuss some of the unintended consequences which may cause more difficult thoughts and feelings to arise, known as 'vicious cycles'.

In Health Psychology, we find this approach especially helpful when there are clear linkages between thoughts, emotions, behaviour and bodily sensations which are important to draw out together with our client (for example adjustment difficulties where low mood or anger about a worsening of condition lead clients to engage in maladaptive coping responses causing more upset). We find it useful to initially discuss a snapshot in time with a client – 'the last time you experienced feeling really fed up about having to take medications', rather than trying to put too much into one five areas formulation.

We include an example of this below in Figure 9.1 for the case example of Anita (Box 9.1). This visualises more clearly than the ABC formulation tool, the cyclical nature of the thoughts, feelings, sensations and coping behaviours that Anita is experiencing around exercise, since it focuses on how the difficult thoughts she is getting lead to scared/panicked feelings, physical symptoms of panic, and avoidance behaviours. These in turn lead to more and a strengthening of those difficult thoughts and the cycle continues. In this case, it may also be useful to supplement the five areas approach with the panic disorder formulation tool (Clark, 1986), since Anita is experiencing thoughts and behaviours associated with panic disorder. Combining the five areas approach with other tools such as the COM-B approach (below) may also help Anita and her psychologist in planning intervention strategies (Table 9.2).

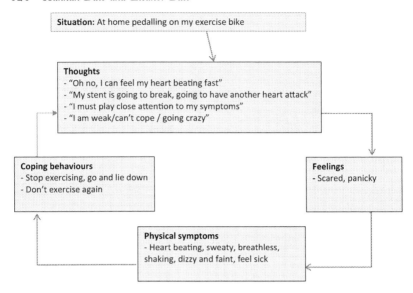

Figure 9.1 CBT five areas formulation example

We would suggest that the five areas approach is most useful where there are clear emotion-driven vicious cycles. Sometimes clients cannot easily identify and label their emotions or would prefer a more all-encompassing approach to identify the many factors impacting on their particular problem (Table 9.2).

Five Ps approach

The five Ps approach to formulation (Kuyken et al, 2009) is another tool commonly applied in CBT. This takes a more longitudinal approach to understanding a client's difficulties. The tool prompts us to explore the *presenting problem*, the *predisposing factors* that may have made someone more likely to experience their problem, the *precipitating factors* that have contributed to this current episode/relapse/concern for their health, the *perpetuating factors* that are keeping the problem going, and the *protective factors* that help support the person to overcome their problems or prevent them from getting worse. This broad tool aids an understanding of the factors affecting the individual's current presentation and indicates areas for intervention, though does not explicitly link to these.

Our fictional scenario John (Box 9.2) is struggling to adjust to his diagnosis of Type 2 diabetes and to make recommended changes to lose

Table 9.2 Formulation tools rated against four considerations for use in clinical practice

Formulation tool	Generalisability	Health comprehensiveness	Accessibility	Link to intervention strategies
ABC functional analysis Examines the function of behaviour through antecedents, behaviour, consequences	Medium Applicable to a range of areas, though specific to exploring antecedents and consequences	High	High	Low Little linkage to intervention planning
ACT case formulation Explores and promotes acceptance of difficult life events and committed action in line with values	High	High	Medium Complex language	Medium Draws out key areas of ACT that are relevant, however doesn't directly link to interventions
CBT five areas Links thoughts, feelings, behaviours and bodily sensations within an individual's situation	High	Low Few prompts to focus on health areas	High	Low Little linkage to intervention planning
CBT five Ps Explores the presenting problem along with predisposing, precipitating, perpetuating and protective factors that are impacting on the individual	High	Medium If tailored towards health beliefs	Medium Complex language	Low Little linkage to intervention planning

(Continued)

Table 9.2 Cont.

Formulation tool	Generalisability	Health comprehensiveness	Accessibility	Link to intervention strategies
COM-B Explores the capability, opportunity and motivation for someone to engage in a behaviour	Medium Focuses more on health behaviour change	High	Medium Some complex language	High
Common sense model Explores the interpretation of symptoms or health information, emotional response and how this affects coping and appraisal	Medium Focuses more on adjustment to physical illness	High	Medium Some complex language	Medium Draws out key adjustment factors, however doesn't directly link to interventions
MAP Explores a person's motivations, actions and prompts around a behaviour	Medium Focuses more on behaviour change	High	High	High
TDF Explores 14 theoretical factors relevant health that may be impacting on an individual	High	High	Low Complex language and many components	High

Transdiagnostic model of adjustment Examines how acute and ongoing illness stressors, along with contextual influences disrupt the equilibrium and feed into cognitive and behavioural responses, which in turn affect adjustment and self-management	Medium Focuses more on adjustment to physical illness	High	Low Some complex language and many components	Medium Draws out key adjustment factors, however doesn't directly link to interventions
TTM Explores stage of change, decisional balance, self-efficacy and 10 processes of change for an individual	Medium Focuses more on behaviour change	High	Medium Some aspects e.g. stage of change easier for people to understand. Other aspects are more complex	Medium Links to 10 intervention strategies, most applicable to behaviour change (rather than adjustment-related distress)

Note: Explanation given where rated as low or medium

weight and start to monitor his blood glucose levels. In Figure 9.2, we have used a combined five Ps and five areas formulation, to demonstrate how two tools can be integrated. The five Ps within this example really focuses on historical factors that have impacted on his presentation, including his family being overweight and also draws out protective factors that may be able to be

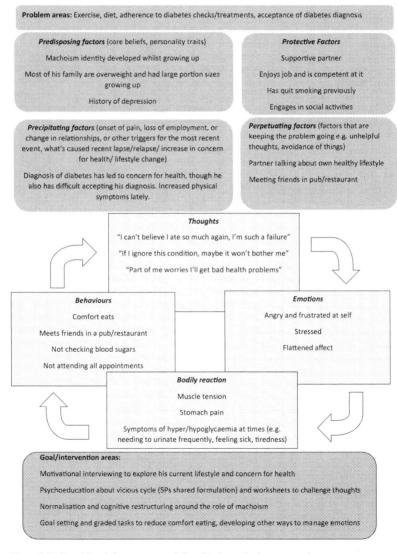

Figure 9.2 Combined five areas and five Ps formulation example

Formulation in clinical practice 129

strengthened to support behaviour change. The five areas in this example additionally offers a snapshot of the vicious cycle of negative thoughts that lead to difficult emotions, bodily sensations and therefore behaviours that perpetuate the difficulties, so it is clear to see how the cycle continues.

We find that a combination of the five areas and five Ps approaches can help us understand the problems as a whole alongside a specific example of how vicious cycles between thoughts, feelings and behaviours are perpetuating the person's difficulties. We would tend to use this combination approach especially where there are several problems which have been troublesome for a long time so that the historical context is key. The five Ps is particularly broad and might be helpful at giving a comprehensive overview of a client's problems. It might need to be used in conjunction with a tool that scores higher on health comprehensiveness and link to intervention strategies in the context of primary prevention and physical health services (Table 9.2).

Acceptance and commitment therapy

Acceptance and commitment therapy (ACT) has been described as belonging to one of the 'third wave' of therapies in the CBT family, following behavioural and traditional cognitive approaches. Instead of identifying and challenging or rationalising unhelpful thinking patterns, acceptance-based approaches such as ACT and mindfulness-based cognitive therapy (Segal et al., 2004) promotes a noticing and accepting approach to difficult thoughts and experiences. ACT in particular aims to help people by promoting awareness of thoughts and feelings surrounding difficult life events and renewing commitment to valued activities in the present moment (Hayes et al., 1999). This is through increasing 'psychological flexibility', a concept that includes six core principles often referred to as the hexaflex: defusion from difficult thoughts, acceptance, mindfulness, the observing self, values, and committed action. Experiential exercises and mindfulness help the client observe their thoughts/feelings to a greater extent in the present moment, accept these rather than struggling or fighting with these and move towards their values-based goals. This formulation and approach can be especially useful for people who have a long-term physical health problem given that there may be much about their health condition that they cannot change, control or predict, and fears about difficult life events (such as worsening health) may well be accurate and cannot be rationalised in the traditional sense.

Figure 9.3 shows an example of a completed ACT hexaflex formulation using the case of Anita. The formulation highlights that Anita is fused with her thoughts which are dominated by worry about the future, rather than being connected with the present moment. Anita is clear that her family and health are of great importance to her, however she is fusing with

Contact with the present moment

How do they connect with the present moment and how often?

Not much. Generally disconnecting with the present moment and worrying about the future lots.

Intervention steps:

Exploring the workability of their worry and teaching mindfulness through collaborating with Anita and trying out different techniques.

Values

What are their core values? Are they living life in line with these?

Discusses family and health as being very important. Somewhat living life to values.

Intervention steps:

Explore other valued areas and use her value of her health to help move her towards taking steps to be more active.

Acceptance/willingness

What could they be more accepting of? What are they already accepting/opening up to?

Accepting of past coronary event but hard to accept future risk and their role in managing that.

Intervention steps:

Explore the short and long term consequences for them and the workability.

Committed actions

What are their goals and have they taken steps towards them?

Tried exercising but chest pain stopped her.

Intervention steps:

Help them move towards increasing exercise gradually, along with engaging more in other valued areas.

Psychological flexibility

Cognitive defusion

What thoughts are they fusing with? When/how are they defusing?

Very fused with thoughts around future health and pain e.g. 'pain means I should stop exercising'

Intervention steps:

Defusion exercises such as hands in front of your face, silly/repetitive voice exercises.

Observer self

Are they able to be an observer? How and when do they manage this?

Not very able to do this.

Intervention steps:

Use experiential exercises to help them develop their observer self, e.g. noticing and labelling thoughts and feelings without judgement, sky/clouds exercise.

Figure 9.3 Acceptance and Commitment Therapy (ACT) formulation example

thoughts that chest pain experienced on exercising is a sign of a heart attack and she should stop. This is contributing to her not being able to take committed action towards a healthy future with her family. The formulation tool helps enable clinicians to explore what intervention approaches from ACT may be useful to use and the completed tool suggests some intervention steps that might be useful for Anita (Table 9.2).

The remaining approaches discussed have been more specifically developed within the Health Psychology field and are typically studied by

Health Psychologists during their training (although not always applied in one-to-one practice work). As such, we find that these tend to be of particular interest to our multidisciplinary team colleagues and team members from other branches of psychology with less of a focus on physical health in their pre-registration training.

The common sense model of self-regulation

The common sense model (CSM) of self-regulation (e.g. Leventhal et al., 1997, 2003), is one of the main theoretical models explaining how people make sense of and psychologically manage challenges to their health. This explores how people interpret symptoms or health information and formulate perceptions of illness and its treatments including their identity, cause, consequences, timeline and curability/control. These perceptions, influenced by emotional responses such as fear and anxiety or depression, influence a person's coping plans (approach and avoidance) appraisal, and responses to feedback. The CSM has been applied to understanding people's experiences in a range of health conditions from heart failure (MacInnes, 2014) to fear of cancer reccurrence (Lee-Jones et al., 1997). Discussing with Health Psychology practitioner colleagues, many find this a useful model for sharing with clients experiencing adjustment difficulties. Figure 9.4 shows how this model could be applied in practice with our case vignette Sinead (Box 9.3), a young woman who is struggling to adjust to a diagnosis of fibromyalgia.

In this model, we can clearly link Sinead's unhelpful beliefs about her diagnosis, unhelpful social messages and interpretation that fibromyalgia is not a real condition contribute to her feelings of anger and shame. These drive some avoidant-focussed coping strategies, resulting in further difficulties for her, which she appraises with some acknowledgement that she would like some help in her coping.

Transdiagnostic model of adjustment

The unified theory of adjustment (Moss-Morris, 2013) and forthcoming updated transdiagnostic model of adjustment in long-term conditions (Moon et al., submitted), also focuses on adjustment to physical health conditions. Building on the CSM and following decades of research and practice by Health Psychology researchers, the transdiagnostic model suggests that the goal of adjustment is maintaining equilibrium. This model proposes that key acute critical events as well as ongoing illness stressors (e.g. diagnosis, threats to health or ongoing management of symptoms) can disrupt equilibrium. A person's response to their initial diagnosis, symptoms and treatment will be influenced by a range of contextual factors (e.g. interpersonal,

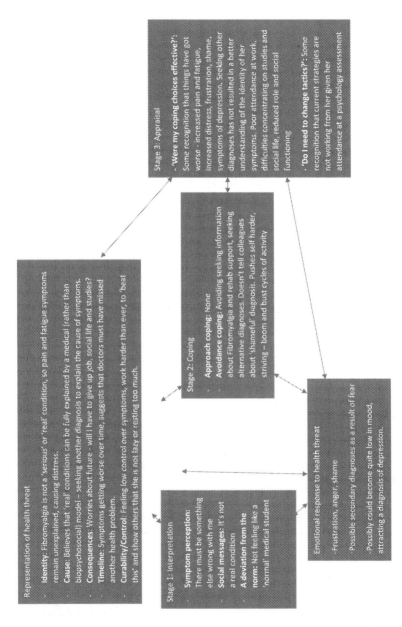

Figure 9.4 Common Sense Model (CSM) formulation example

environmental and illness-specific factors) which need to be considered in helping people return to equilibrium. Returning to equilibrium and good psychological, social and physical adjustment also depends on cognitive and behavioural factors, such as a person's self-efficacy surrounding disease management and use of problem-focused coping strategies. Together the model aims to explain why some people adjust well to health conditions and others struggle, experiencing distress and functional difficulties. Figure 9.5 displays this visually.

In the case of Sinead (Figure 9.5), we may formulate that the misperceptions and stigma surrounding Fibromyalgia that she had absorbed during her medical degree fuelled strong emotions of shame and anger on diagnosis. She responded to this disequilibrium by using her usual coping strategy of hard work, pushing herself harder than ever, to prove to herself and others that she did not fit the stigmatising label she had been offered. A Health Psychologist working with Sinead could use the formulation to gently unpack and challenge some of the misconceived beliefs Sinead had around fibromyalgia and offer Sinead some understanding around boom-and-bust cycles in pain and fatigue. It would be important that the Health Psychologist would not try to convince Sinead to 'accept' the diagnosis, which she experiences as stigmatising, as this would likely rupture their therapeutic relationship. Instead, it would be important for the Health Psychologist to work with Sinead on her own goals of learning strategies to help her do the things that are most important to her, despite pain and fatigue.

We feel this model is valuable in characterising adjustment clearly and the balancing analogy helpful in explaining why adjustment is a continual process in the face of events and stressors, rather than a one-off 'acceptance' which happens on diagnosis. It also points to cognitive and behavioural strategies which could form the basis of an intervention plan, strengths summarised in Table 9.2. The authors advise that when used in practice, this model would be valuable to guide a psychologist's own formulation and intervention, but recommend using the five areas or another approach when sharing formulations with clients (Susan Carroll, 17 March 2021, personal communication).

Motivation, action, prompts model

The motivation, action, prompts (MAP) model (Dixon & Johnston, 2020a) was developed by Health Psychologists seconded to The Scottish Government as a theory-based mnemonic for helping non-specialist practitioners to select behaviour change techniques to use with their clients (Michie et al., 2013). This discusses motivation development, action control, and

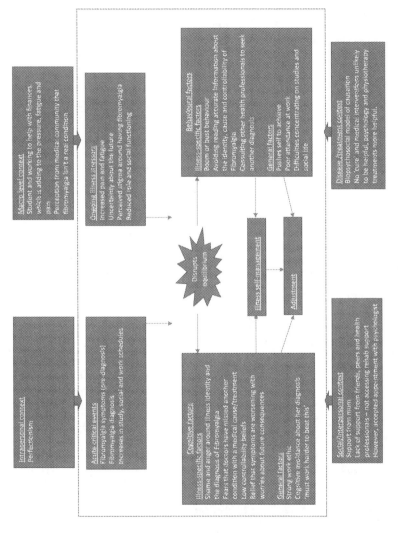

Figure 9.5 Transdiagnostic model of adjustment formulation example

prompts and cues as three routes to changing behaviours (e.g. increasing inhaler use). In our clinical practice we have found it helpful to develop a formulation tool version of MAP, illustrated in Figure 9.6, which we feel can be readily applied to work in primary preventive and physical health services.

Figure 9.6 presents a formulation of John's case using the MAP approach. In addition to what is drawn out from the five areas and five Ps tools, this highlights his ambivalence to change and current low intentions to change, along with a more detailed understanding of how environmental prompts are impacting on his behaviour. It also better indicates what might be included in a treatment plan (including what to target first), including motivational interviewing, goal setting and restructuring the environment. As summarised in Table 9.2, while focussed purely on routes to change, we feel this tool has high acceptability in client work and readily links with intervention strategies.

The capability, opportunity, motivation – behaviour model

The capability, opportunity, motivation – behaviour (COM-B) model forms the hub of the behaviour change wheel for intervention development, a hugely influential Health Psychology model again developed primarily to aid non-specialists to use psychological theory in practice (Michie et al., 2014). COM-B explains that for behaviour change to occur, people must have capability (knowledge and skills, both physical and psychological), opportunity (a supportive social and physical environment), and motivation (both automatic motivation such as habits and drives, and more reflective motivation considering pros and cons).

While most often used to understand and change behaviour at the group or population level, we have found the model useful in our work with clients and have developed tool outlines with the three (e.g. heading 'motivation') or six components (e.g. headings 'reflective motivation' and 'automatic motivation'). As discussed in Table 9.2, compared to traditional CBT formulation approaches, COM-B more explicitly discusses behaviour change and intervention planning, including prompting the psychologist to think about which approaches to focus on first with clients. We find COM-B to be particularly useful in primary prevention services, where the remit is often more purely focussed on behaviour change (at various levels of complexity, discussed in Figure 9.9). The TDF (described below) offers consideration of a greater range of factors that might be very helpful to understanding a client's adjustment to their health condition, in physical health services. As such, the case example we present for the case vignette of John uses a combined COM-B and TDF approach (Figure 9.7).

Target behaviour(s):	Exercise, diet, adherence to diabetes checks/treatments, adjustment to diabetes diagnosis		
MAP Route to Behaviour Change	Detail the key factors that are affecting behaviour for your client (this could be based on the frequency of barriers in this area, the likely positive impact of change in that area, their wish for help in this area and your judgement of what help you can offer)	Detail the Key BCTs you will use to target with the aim of behaviour change (think about the kinds of BCTs and other approaches (not listed as BCTs) you will use to support your chosen domains and how you might go about delivering them)	Further details of techniques used (*star or underline any to focus on initially)
Motivation	Appears ambivalent about making any changes to manage his diabetes (exercise, diet, adherence). Some machoism affecting this and feeding into denial. Pattern of emotional eating fed by negative thoughts and emotions. Not able to acknowledge potential consequences of diabetes, particularly if not well managed. Overall, no current intentions to change.	• Motivational Interviewing (MI) • Information about health consequences • Reduce negative emotions • Normalisation • Psychoeducation • Social support (unspecified)	• MI to explore his ambivalence to change and his knowledge of consequences and provide this within an elicit-provide-elicit (EPE) framework. May incorporate 2 futures exercise and pros and cons exercise* • Build ways to manage emotions other than through the use of comfort eating e.g. though talking to others, relaxation, engagement with enjoyable activities, mindfulness, and general stress management*

Formulation in clinical practice 137

- Normalisation of diabetes diagnosis appearing as a threat to male identity and psychoeducation around how being brought up in a 'macho' environment may have contributed*
- Encouragement to discuss his diagnosis with others and to mentally challenge threats to identity*
- Raise awareness of the cycle of physiological symptoms, thoughts, emotions and behaviour and intervene to break it through raising awareness of automatic thoughts, thought diaries, developing balanced/alternative thoughts and through behavioural changes
- Goal setting using graded tasks, and drawing on problem solving, action planning and implementation intentions where relevant
- Develop rewards he can give himself upon completion of behavioural goals

Action | Hasn't yet taken any steps or set goals | Only once more motivated:
- Goal setting (behaviour)
- Problem solving
- Action planning
- Graded tasks
- Self-monitoring of lifestyle through a food and physical activity diary (linked to emotions)
- Review behavioural goal(s)
- Self-incentive

| Prompts | Prompts in the environment support high fat and sugar diet – social prompts when out with friends, availability of food at home and work | Only once more motivated:
• Restructuring the physical environment
• Restructuring the social environment
• Avoidance/reducing exposure to cues for the behaviour
• Social support (practical)
• Adding objects to the environment
• Distraction | • Change the availability of high fat and sugar foods in the house through changing what is bought and through switching to online shopping to avoid unintentional buying in shops
• Reduce the number of times he meets friends at pubs and restaurants each week to avoid social cues to eating/drinking
• Support him to discuss with friends encouraging him to eat more healthily/drink less
• Buy more low fat and sugar foods and take them to work and be visible at home to prompt consumption
• Plan other interests to focus on during work breaks other than food |

Figure 9.6 Motivation, Action Prompts (MAP) model formulation example

Formulation in clinical practice 139

TDF and COM-B Integrated Formulation Tool

Target behaviour(s):		Exercise, diet, adherence to diabetes checks/treatments, adjustment to diabetes diagnosis		
COM-B Component, *Definition*	TDF Domain, *Definition* and (Constructs in brackets)	Detail the key TDF domains that are relevant for your client (this could be based on the frequency of barriers in this domain, the likely positive impact of change in that area, their wish for help in this area and your judgement of what help you can offer)	Key BCTs (think about the kinds of BCTs and other approaches (not listed as BCTs) you will use to support your chosen domains and how you might go about delivering them)	Further details of techniques used (*star or underline any to focus on initially)
Physical Capability, *Physical skill, strength or stamina*	Skills *An ability or proficiency acquired through practice* (Skills, Skills development, Competence Ability, Interpersonal skills, Practice, Skill assessment)	• Does not yet have the stamina/skills required to increase exercise • Isn't aware of blood sugar levels due to lack of monitoring/skills to do so	• Graded tasks • Action planning • Self-monitoring of outcome(s) of behaviour • Rewards	• Focus on 'steps in the right direction' • Planning small achievable goals to build stamina/skills • Rewards for successfully monitoring blood sugars • Modelling of and behavioural practice of checking blood (in different situations)

| Psychological Capability
Knowledge or psychological skills, strength or stamina to engage in the necessary mental processes | Knowledge
An awareness of the existence of something (Knowledge (including knowledge of condition/scientific rationale), Procedural knowledge, knowledge of task environment) | • Good knowledge of what he needs to do but not of the behavioural steps that might be required | • Motivational interviewing (MI)
• Psychoeducation
• Behavioural experiments | • MI to explore his knowledge further and provide psychoeducation of the biopsychosocial steps required for behaviour change within an elicit-provide-elicit (EPE) framework*

• Behavioural experiments to test out whether he can make changes by using non-specific plans (if there is resistance to action planning/implementation intentions) |
| | Memory, attention and decision processes
The ability to retain information, focus selectively on aspects of the environment and choose between two or more alternatives (Memory, Attention, Attention control, Decision making, Cognitive overload/tiredness) | • No cognitive or attention impairments | | |

Formulation in clinical practice 141

Behavioural regulation *Anything aimed at managing or changing objectively observed or measured actions)* Self-monitoring, Breaking habit, Action planning	Not currently monitoring glucose levels or diet/physical activity	• Self-monitoring of behaviour • Self-monitoring of outcome(s) of behaviour • Biofeedback • Goal setting (behaviour) • Action planning	• Self-monitoring of lifestyle through a food and physical activity diary (linked to emotions) • Use of glucose monitoring to assess the outcomes of behaviour • Goal setting and action planning (implementation intentions) to support changes
Physical Opportunity *Opportunity afforded by the environment involving time, resources, locations, cues, physical* Environmental context and resources *Any circumstance of a person's situation or environment that discourages or encourages the development of skills and abilities, independence, social competence and adaptive behaviour (Environmental stressors, Resources/material resources, Organisational culture/climate, Salient events/critical incidents, Person × environment interaction, Barriers and facilitators)*	• Good availability of high fat and sugar foods at home and at work • Meets friends at pubs and restaurants and generally gets high fat and sugar meals, along with alcohol	• Restructuring the physical environment • Restructuring the social environment • Avoidance/reducing exposure to cues for the behaviour • Adding objects to the environment • Distraction	• Change the availability of high fat and sugar foods in the house through changing what is bought and through switching to online shopping to avoid unintentional buying in shops • Reduce the number of times he meets friends at pubs and restaurants each week to avoid social cues to eating/drinking • Buy more low fat and sugar foods and take them to work and be visible at home to prompt consumption • Plan other interests to focus on during work breaks other than food

Social Opportunity *Opportunity afforded by interpersonal influences, social cues and cultural norms that influence the way that we think about things*	Social influences *Those interpersonal processes that can cause individuals to change their thoughts, feelings, or behaviours* Social pressure, Social norms, Group conformity, Social comparisons, Group norms, Social support, Power, Intergroup conflict, Alienation, Group identity, Modelling	• Supportive partner, however sometimes talks too much about how they have been active and have lost weight, which can be disincentivising • Influence of friends he meets can mean he eats more when out with them	• Social support (unspecified) • Social support (practical) • Avoidance/reducing exposure to cues for the behaviour	• Ask partner to be supportive of changes by giving appropriate praise (and avoiding their own self-praise), along with also purchasing low fat and sugar foods • Reduce the number of times he meets friends at pubs and restaurants each week to avoid social cues to eating • Support him to discuss with friends encouraging him to eat more healthily/drink less
Reflective Motivation *Reflective processes involving plans (self-conscious intentions) and evaluations (beliefs about what is good and bad)*	Professional/social role and identity *A coherent set of behaviours and displayed personal qualities of an individual in a social or work setting* (Professional identity, Professional role, Social identity, Identity, Professional boundaries, Professional confidence, Group identity, Leadership, Organisational commitment)	• Strong professional identity as an IT manager/leader • Slight machoism	• Normalisation • Psychoeducation • Social support (unspecified) • Behavioural practice/rehearsal (role play) • Incompatible beliefs • Identity associated with changed behaviour	• Normalisation of diabetes diagnosis appearing as a threat to identity and psychoeducation around how being brought up in a 'macho' environment may have contributed* • Encouragement to discuss his diagnosis with others and to mentally challenge threats to identity* • Role play how he might discuss his diagnosis and need to check bloods/make lifestyle changes with others

Formulation in clinical practice 143

Beliefs about capabilities *Acceptance of the truth, reality or validity about an ability, talent or facility that a person can put to constructive use* (Self-confidence, Perceived competence, Self-efficacy, Perceived behavioural control, Beliefs, Self-esteem, Empowerment, Professional confidence)	• Partially struggling to accept his diagnosis, though is able to discuss it • Shows some self-efficacy about potential change, however is non-specific about behaviours he would enact to achieve change	• Normalisation • Psychoeducation • Exploration of beliefs • Framing/reframing • Action planning • Problem solving • Graded tasks • Motivational interviewing • Focus on past success	• Elicit or highlight how his strong identity conflicts with not making changes to support the management of his diabetes and support the construction of an identity where behaviour change aligns with this* • Normalisation of the difficulty people face on receiving a new diagnosis and psychoeducation about adjustment processes* • Exploration of beliefs about what it means to have diabetes and prompt the reframing of his diagnosis as something from which positive change can come* • Build self-efficacy to achieve specific behavioural goals (including checking bloods) though graded tasks, action planning and implementation intentions • Modelling and behavioural practice of checking blood (in different situations)* • MI, including the use of affirmations to support self-efficacy following achievement of any goal, and drawing on past successes

Optimism *The confidence that things will happen for the best or that desired goals will be attained* (Optimism, Pessimism, Unrealistic optimism, Identity)	• Feels that it's unlikely that he'll develop complications as he's young (unrealistic optimism)	• Motivational Interviewing • Information about health consequences	• MI to explore his knowledge of consequences and provide this within an elicit-provide-elicit (EPE) framework*
Beliefs about consequences *Acceptance of the truth, reality, or validity about outcomes of a behaviour in a given situation* (Beliefs, Outcome expectancies, Characteristics of outcome expectancies, Anticipated regret, Consequents)	• Generally feels that he will not develop any life-affecting consequences from his diabetes	• Motivational interviewing • Comparative imagining of future outcomes • Anticipated regret • Paradoxical instructions • Self-monitoring • Information about emotional consequences • Information about antecedents • Information about health consequences • Information about social and environmental consequences	• 2 futures exercise within an MI approach* • Prompt discussion around anticipated regret should he not attempt any changes* • Used within an MI approach (and cautiously at the right time), advise him that he may as well keep eating, not engaging in physical activity and not engage in self-management behaviours (paradoxical instructions)* • Support self-monitoring of blood sugars (once some of the barriers listed elsewhere have been worked on) and self-monitoring of emotional consequences of physical activity and health heating

Formulation in clinical practice   145

Intentions *A conscious decision to perform a behaviour or a resolve to act in a certain way* (Stability of intentions, Stages of change model, Transtheoretical model and stages of change)	• No current intention to change, however shows ambivalence – contemplation	• Motivational interviewing • Pros and cons	• Using an MI approach, explore the biopsychosocial consequences of his current lifestyle behaviours and lack of self-management (may include the use of a 5 areas formulation) • MI to explore his ambivalence about change; may include pros and cons exercise*
Goals *Mental representations of outcomes or end states that an individual wants to achieve* (Goals (distal/proximal), Goal priority, Goal/target setting, Goals (autonomous/controlled), Action planning, Implementation intention)	• No current goals	• Goal setting (behaviour) • Problem solving • Action planning • Review behavioural goal(s) • Self-incentive	• Goal setting using graded tasks, and drawing on problem solving, action planning and implementation intentions where relevant • Develop rewards he can give himself upon completion of behavioural goals

Automatic Motivation	Reinforcement	Current reinforcement of some unhealthy eating habits through comfort eating and enjoyable meals at restaurants	• Reduce negative emotions • Goal setting (behaviour) • Problem solving • Self-incentive	• Build ways to manage emotions other than through the use of comfort eating e.g. though talking to others, relaxation, engagement with enjoyable activities, mindfulness, and general stress management* • Setting goals and exploring coping planning for choosing lower fat and sugar options in restaurants • Develop rewards he can give himself upon completion of behavioural goals
Automatic processes involving emotional reactions, desires (wants and needs), impulses, inhibitions, drive states and reflex responses	*Increasing the probability of a response by arranging a dependent relationship, or contingency, between the response and a given stimulus* (Rewards (proximal/distal, valued/not valued, probable/improbable), Incentives, Punishment, Consequents, Reinforcement, Contingencies, Sanctions)			
	Emotion	Clear pattern of physiological symptoms, thoughts, emotions and behaviour reinforcing eating habits, including emotional eating (see 5 areas formulation tool for greater detail)	• Reduce negative emotions • Information about antecedents	• Build ways to manage emotions e.g. though talking to others, relaxation, engagement with enjoyable activities, mindfulness, and general stress management* • Raise awareness of the cycle of physiological symptoms, thoughts, emotions and behaviour and intervene to break it through raising awareness of automatic thoughts, thought diaries, developing balanced/alternative thoughts and through behavioural changes
	A complex reaction pattern, involving experiential, behavioural, and physiological elements, by which the individual attempts to deal with a personally significant matter or event (Fear, Anxiety, Affect, Stress, Depression, Positive/negative affect, Burn-out)			

Transtheoretical Model Formulation tool

Behaviour change discussed: Dietary and exercise changes

Stage of change (mark where the patient is on the stages of change)

| Pre-contemplation | <u>Contemplation</u> | Preparation | Action | Maintenance |

Detail their decisional balance (This may be completed just for behaviour or for behaviour change, or both. It can be helpful to think about the short and long term)

Pros of current behaviour	Cons of current behaviour	Cons of behaviour change	Pros of behaviour change
Enjoys food, including the social side and some comfort eating	Short term: poor management of diabetes	Doesn't have the stamina to exercise	Better management of diabetes
	Long term: may lead to diabetes complications	Feels has been managing ok so far and diabetes markers are not too bad	Reduced risk of diabetic complications
		Feels any changes may be unnecessary as is fairly young so thinks complications less likely	May help manage stress

Self efficacy (rate their self efficacy for engaging in their new behaviour (behaviour change)

I am confident in my ability to [insert behaviour]

| Strongly disagree | Disagree | <u>Neither agree nor disagree</u> | agree | Strongly agree |

Processes of change (detail where the person is at for the 10 processes and the intervention steps that could be taken)

Cognitive/affective processes | Intervention steps (this may be through finding ways to increase their self-efficacy, further support the processes of change, or if utilising integrative formulation/interventions, come from a range of behaviour change techniques):

1. Consciousness Raising:
Has a good understanding of the diet and exercise behaviours that support diabetes.

2. Dramatic Relief:
Understands the potential negative consequences, however has unrealistic optimism (feels it's unlikely to happen to him).

Use motivational interviewing to explore the potential negative consequences.

3. Environmental re-evaluation:
Understands that his lack of exercise can lead to some conflict with his partner, and how both behaviours impact on his health.

Help him identify how his partner could be helpful and discuss/practice how he might discuss the challenges with her.

4. Self-re-evaluation:
Slight machoism and strong identity as an IT manager barriers to change.

5. Social Liberation:
Feels that his meals at the pub are an integral part of how he fits in with friends/society.

Explore with him how his identity/machoism and views about friends/society (social liberation) may be barriers to change and use normalisation and psychoeducation about culture to help him shift this a little and accept that good diabetes management can fit with these.

See self-re-evaluation.

Behavioural processes | Intervention steps:

6. Self-Liberation:
Currently, not committed to change.

Once he has moved more towards the preparation stage, further support self-liberation through affirmations, draw on past successes to increase self-efficacy.

7. Counter Conditioning:
Not currently engaging in healthier behaviours (or healthier thoughts).

8. Helping Relationships:
Has a supportive partner, however the support isn't always perceived as helpful.

9. Reinforcement Management:
Some alleviation of negative emotions through comfort eating.

10. Stimulus Control:
Meeting friends in a pub is a prompt for his unhealthy eating
Availability of unhealthy foods and focus on food in work breaks unhelpful.

Use positive self-talk, graded tasks, action planning and implementation intentions to help support steps to behaviour change.

Help him identify and use social support from partner and friends to support behaviour change.

Support him to develop ways other than comfort eating of managing negative emotions, including exercise, relaxation and engagement in other enjoyable activities. Build in rewards for achieving steps towards his healthy eating and exercise goals.

Cut down on the number of times he meets friends at pubs and restaurants each week to avoid social cues to eating/drinking. Switch to online shopping to avoid unintentional buying in shops and shift the availability of high fat and sugar foods in the house to low fat and sugar foods. Take healthier snacks to work and find other interests to engage in in work breaks other than food.

Figure 9.8 Transtheoretical model (TTM) formulation example

Theoretical domains framework

Theoretical domains framework (TDF) is a theory-based approach developed to bring together and group 14 domains of psychological influences on behaviour from different theories that encompass cognitions, affect, social and environmental determinants (Atkins et al., 2017; Cane et al., 2012; Michie et al., 2005). This comprehensive and systematically developed approach can prompt a psychologist to think through which determinants of behaviours may be relevant for their client and how these link to BCTs (Michie et al., 2011). It also prompts the psychologist to think about the specific approach they will use to implement a BCT (or other approach), along with which ones they will focus on initially (i.e. if the client is ambivalent towards making changes, exploring their motivation and other barriers rather than jumping to goal setting).

Our tool in Figure 9.7 adapts the original framework slightly for use with one-to-one clients. This is presented below applied to our case example John (Box 9.2). This tool draws out more depth around the complex factors impacting on his adjustment and behaviour than are captured by the other tools. For example, his identity as an IT manager/leader, his wavering self-efficacy and his health optimism. The TDF may, therefore, be especially useful at drawing out the complexities involved and/or where there are a large number of behavioural constructs impacting on an individual's behaviour or adjustment to a physical health condition. It may be especially relevant when supporting adjustment to and coping with physical health conditions. However, we tend to find it is less accessible when doing shared formulation work with clients (see Table 9.2).

Transtheoretical model

The transtheoretical model (TTM) (Prochaska & DiClemente, 1983; Prochaska, DiClemente & Norcross, 1992) aims to be broad in its approach to understanding behaviour and indicating intervention approaches that may be effective. It includes four elements. The first, most commonly used is the stages of change, which suggests that people move through different stages towards a behaviour: pre-contemplation, contemplation, preparation, action, maintenance (and sometimes relapse/termination). The second is decisional balance, which enables a person to weight up the pros and cons of engaging in a certain behaviour, or in a behaviour change. Where a person is struggling to understand 'pros and cons', we have found it helpful to frame these as 'positives and negatives'. Self-efficacy brings in elements from Bandura's self-efficacy theory, exploring the person's self-efficacy for undertaking a behaviour (Bandura, 1977, 1982). Finally, there are 10 processes of change, which describe five key cognitive/affective processes that are generally considered to happen earlier in the behaviour change process, and five behavioural processes that support behaviour change later on in the behaviour change process. While the model is therefore complex and multi-faceted, stages of change are frequently used as a stand-alone concept, despite limited evidence that tailoring interventions to a client's stage of change is effective (e.g. West, 2005). We would strongly recommend psychologists use a fuller version of the TTM if using this model in clinical practice.

Figure 9.8 shows how the TTM can be applied in a formulation tool, which focused specifically on the dietary and physical activity behaviours that are impacting on John's diabetes (rather than the further adjustment and diabetes testing difficulties that are also present). This tool points to John experiencing the contemplation stage of change, at times thinking about the pros and cons of his current behaviour. The example suggests that to promote change, his self-efficacy needs strengthening and summarises the 10 processes. The processes clearly help link to intervention strategies, first focusing on cognitive/affective strategies (e.g. gently exploring the negative consequences, and normalisation/psychoeducation around the impact of machoism-type identity beliefs), then moving onto behavioural strategies (e.g. implementation intentions and reducing social cues to eating unhealthy foods). We find this tool may be useful when focusing on a specific behaviour(s) but also where it is clear that cognitive/affective processes are clearly influencing the behaviour (that may not be so readily captured by tools such as the COM-B or MAP).

Picking a tool to use

As can be seen from the case vignette examples, there is clear overlap between the information and sense-making in the 10 tools we have discussed. This is unsurprising given that the key origins for all of these tools arise from common psychological principles, theories, therapeutic approaches and evidence. Sometimes the differences lie in semantics and structure rather than essence or underlying psychological principles. However, in thinking about which tool to use in clinical practice, we would consider all to have strengths and weaknesses.

In reflecting on our practice experiences, we think these vary on four main dimensions which may help psychologists choose a tool: *generalisability* to a wide range of different problems; *health comprehensiveness* involving theory and practice which considers factors relevant to primary prevention and/or physical health services; how much the tool helps a clinician *link to intervention strategies*; and *accessibility* for shared formulation with clients (i.e.

how easy is it for a client to understand). Table 9.2 includes our own ratings of these formulation approaches to help summarise and guide clinicians to what tool(s) may be useful for their clients and services. The 10 approaches are presented in alphabetical order.

We find these tools can be used individually or integratively (using two or more tools to help formulate what's going on for one person), depending on what feels most useful for the psychologist and client and depending on 'complexity' (see section below). As discussed, when primary (or secondary) prevention and coping with a physical health condition are both areas for intervention, it may be useful to combine, for instance a five Ps formulation to understand the coping challenges with MAP, COM-B or TDF to fully consider their impact on health-related behaviours. A further important consideration is clinician training and familiarity with the theory/model that the tool is drawing on. For example, for someone unfamiliar with the TDF, substantial reading or training would be required to accurately formulate using this model.

Shared formulations

We have found most of the tools to be compatible with collaboratively, co-creating formulations with our clients. To engage clients in this process and help to make the tools accessible, we try to adopt a motivational interviewing approach (Miller & Rollnick, 2012). For instance, we provide our understanding of different parts of the formulation using the elicit–provide–elicit technique for giving information, frequently check understandings, trying to avoid psychological jargon and above all ensuring that the client feels the expert in their lives and sense making. In a face-to-face session, we may present a blank diagram and encourage the client to do the writing. Several of the tools such as COM-B can be used in a more elaborate (six-component) or summary (three-component) way, depending on what is most suitable for the client. The transdiagnostic model of adjustment, TDF and TTM formulations are likely too complex to feedback in their full forms to most clients, therefore they are likely useful tools for a clinician but may need to be summarised a bit more simply, or the key factors that are relevant to that client drawn out. Indeed, the authors of the transdiagnostic model of adjustment advise that it may be useful to share some of these broader aspects of the model with the person to help them to make sense of and validate their experiences. However, they advise to do this verbally as mapping out the whole model might be confusing (Carroll, personal communication). In their paper, Moon et al. (submitted) suggest using the CBT five areas model as a more simple and digestible tool in a shared formulation. In a remote working scenario, it might be helpful to share the formulation before or after a session via email or post, with a verbal discussion in the session. If video conferencing software is being used, screen sharing could facilitate the visual sharing of a formulation during a session, which might aid the understanding by an individual.

When the process of shared formulation goes well, clients feel relieved, rather than overwhelmed to get a better sense of why they're struggling with something and can start to notice vicious cycles where their thinking patterns or behaviours may keep them stuck. Sometimes this awareness is enough for clients to take the next step in helping them become unstuck. In other cases, we find it important that discussions about formulations include the psychologist offering the client hope that through this better understanding, they can work together to find what is changeable (among what isn't, such as their physical health symptoms) to live life better.

Complexity in assessment, formulation and treatment planning

In this final section, we turn to defining and working with cases with more complexity, since this is a term we find often used in psychological services. A thorough and well-grounded assessment and formulation is particularly important with more 'complex' cases. However, there can be no single straightforward definition of 'complexity' within one-to-one Health Psychology work. It would be stigmatising to categorise a person as 'complex', since an individual's needs change over time and the factors which make someone 'complex' are often outside of their control. Several elements may be indicative of a more complex presentation which would tend to require a more intense, multi-component assessment and formulation and tailored, possibly longer-term intervention. Existing stepped care/tiered models for psychological therapy (e.g. NHS Health Scotland, 2019; Scottish Government, 2018) often position those with the most severe mental health problems as being the most complex cases, but we would argue this doesn't encapsulate complexity well in primary prevention and physical health services. Distress and a previous mental health history would certainly be part of complexity, but this would also depend on, for example, the extent of their physical health comorbidities, life-limiting nature of their condition, the demands of their regimen, their distress levels and a previous mental health history, interacting psychological influences, the length of time they have been struggling with a problem, their range of and attachment to their health beliefs, factors impacting on self-efficacy and experiences of social support or stigma, or socio-structural inequalities which impact on the ability to engage the client.

Understanding such physical health complexities and considerations around psychological adjustment are critical in assessment, formulation and treatment planning. In our case formulations in this chapter, we feel that in order to help John (who may not meet criteria for a diagnosable mental health condition), interventions would require a more integrative formulation and multi-component treatment plan than Anita, who is experiencing symptoms of panic disorder. Similarly, we find equal biopsychosocial complexities when working with individuals around primary prevention without a current long-term condition, such as when working in primary care or looked-after children's services.

We would propose a new tiered model of 'complexity' within assessment, formulation and interventions in Health Psychology clinical practice (Figure 9.9, below). Health Psychologists will likely be involved in designing Tier 1 and 2 programmes, along with delivering training and supervision for other staff delivering interventions at that level. However, their direct client contact would most likely come under Tiers 3 and 4, offering specialist psychological input to support self-management and wellbeing. It is of course, vital that as autonomous HCPC-registered Health Psychologists, we practice within our competency area, engaging in regular supervision and taking continuing professional development opportunities.

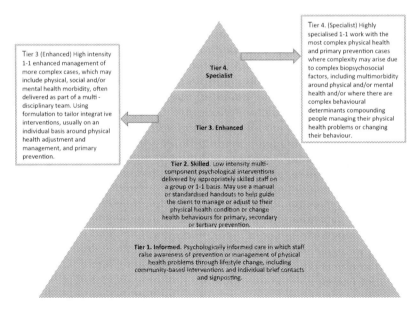

Figure 9.9 Stepped care model of psychological interventions in health psychology clinical practice

In our view, psychological services in physical health settings should be focussed on the shared multi-disciplinary team goals of adjustment and self-management for health, for instance, helping people with self-management difficulties with emotional distress that is related to their physical health condition. This would be in contrast to more siloed work to treat distress in isolation from physical health, which tends to improve distress with little impact on self-management and therefore medical outcomes (e.g. Gonzalez et al., 2015). If a person presents with emotional distress that appears unrelated to (e.g. pre-dates and they feel is separate to) their health condition, they may be better served by their local primary care mental health service. This ensures a clear remit for psychologists within clinical health settings.

Conclusion

In this chapter we have aimed to present a practical overview of formulation in Health Psychology clinical practice. This is based on our own practice in a wide range of settings, but is by no means the 'one true path' to (assessment and) formulation. We have presented the tools that we have found most useful in our clinical practice and the considerations that may be important in choosing a tool to use. A range of tools have been presented and although this doesn't cover every theory/model that a Health Psychologist may draw on, we hope that the demonstration of the use of these within clinical practice may aid people to develop their own tools based on other approaches. Four approaches presented derive from the 'three waves' of CBT which all psychological practitioners will learn about in their pre-registration training. Six others are more commonly included in Health Psychologists' pre-registration training and are usually a specialist area of expertise brought by Health Psychologists in multi-disciplinary teams. We have also presented a new tiered model of work within primary prevention and physical health services, which we feel encapsulates the complexities that are seen within Health Psychology clinical practice. Further work would be useful to develop and evaluate the use of the formulation tools, in line with theory and evidence, including integrating multiple tools. We would also hope to more systematically develop Table 9.2 over time, conducting research to explore the domains that best capture psychologists' experience using formulation in one-to-one client work. We would be pleased to hear from other Health Psychologists working in these areas and perhaps build an open access online repository of psychologists' formulation tools for interested members of our community to explore.

References

Atkins, L., Francis, J., Islam, R., O'Connor, D., Patey, A., Ivers, N., ... & Michie, S. (2017). A guide to using the Theoretical Domains Framework of behaviour change to investigate implementation problems. *Implementation Science*, 12(1), 1–18.

Bandura, A. (1977). Self-efficacy: Toward a unifying theory of behavioral change. *Psychological Review*, 84, 191–215.

Bandura, A. (1982). Self-efficacy mechanism in human agency. *American Psychologist*, 37(2), 122.

Beck, A.T. (1967). *Depression: Clinical, experimental and theoretical aspects*. New York: Harper & Row.

British Psychological Society. (2011). *Good practice guidelines on the use of psychological formulation*. Leicester: British Psychological Society.

British Psychological Society. (2015). *Qualification in Health Psychology (Stage 2) candidate handbook*. Leicester: British Psychological Society.

Butler, G. (1998). Clinical formulation. In A.S. Bellack & M. Hersen (eds), *Comprehensive clinical psychology*. Oxford: Pergamon.

Cane, J., O'Connor, D., & Michie, S. (2012). Validation of the theoretical domains framework for use in behaviour change and implementation research. *Implementation Science*, 7(1), 1–17.

Clark, D. M. (1986). A cognitive approach to panic. *Behaviour Research and Therapy*, 24(4), 461–470.

Craig, P., Dieppe, P., Macintyre, S., Michie, S., Nazareth, I., & Petticrew, M. (2008). Developing and evaluating complex interventions: the Medical Research Council guidance. Retrieved from https://mrc.ukri.org/documents/pdf/complex-interventions-guidance/.

Dixon, D., & Johnston, M. (2010). *Health behaviour change competency framework: Competences to deliver interventions to change lifestyle behaviours that affect health*. Edinburgh: Scottish Government.

Dixon, D., & Johnston, M. (2020a). MAP: A mnemonic for mapping BCTs to three routes to behaviour change. *British Journal of Health Psychology*, 25(4), 1086–1101.

Dixon, D., & Johnston, M. (2020b). What competences are required to deliver person-person behaviour change interventions: Development of a health behaviour change competency framework. *International Journal of Behavioral Medicine*, 1–10. doi:10.1007/s12529-020-09920-6.

Engel, G.L. (1980). The clinical application of the biopsychosocial model. *American Journal of Psychiatry*, 137(5), 535–544.

Gonzalez, J. S., Shreck, E., Psaros, C., & Safren, S. A. (2015). Distress and type 2 diabetes-treatment adherence: A mediating role for perceived control. *Health Psychology*, 34(5), 505.

Hayes, S. C., Strosahl, K., & Wilson, K. G. (1999). *Acceptance and commitment therapy: An experiential approach to behaviour change*. New York: Guilford Press.

Health and Care Professions Council. (2015). *Standards of proficiency: Practitioner psychologists*. London: Health and Care Professions Council.

Health Education England. (2021). Behaviour change development framework. Retrieved from https://behaviourchange.hee.nhs.uk.

Hilton, C. E., & Johnston, L. H. (2017). Health Psychology: It's not what you do, it's the way that you do it. *Health Psychology Open*, 4(2).
Johnston, M. (2016). What more can we learn from early learning theory? The contemporary relevance for behaviour change interventions. *British Journal of Health Psychology*, 21(1), 1–10. doi:10.1111/bjhp.12165.
Johnstone, L., & Dallos, R. (2013). *Formulation in psychology and psychotherapy: Making sense of people's problems*. New York: Routledge.
Kuyken, W., Padesky, C. A., & Dudley, R. (2009). *Collaborative case conceptualization: Working effectively with clients in cognitive-behavioral therapy*. New York: Guilford Press.
Lee-Jones C, Humphris G, Dixon R, et al. (1997) Fear of cancer recurrence: A literature review and formulation to explain exacerbation of recurrence fears. *Psycho-Oncology*, 6(2), 95–105.
Leventhal, H., Benyamini, Y., Brownlee, S., Diefenbach, M., Leventhal, E., Patrick-Miller, L., & Robitaille, C. (1997). Illness representations: Theoretical foundations. In K. J. Petrie & J. Weinman (eds), *Perceptions of health and illness: Current research and applications* (pp. 19–45). London: Harwood.
Leventhal, H., Brissette, I., & Leventhal, E. A. (2003). The common-sense model of self-regulation of health and illness. In L. D. Cameron & H. Leventhal (Eds.), *The self-regulation of health and illness behaviour* (p. 42–65). New York: Routledge.
MacInnes, J. (2014). An exploration of illness representations and treatment beliefs in heart failure. *Journal of clinical nursing*, 23(9–10),1249–1256.
Michie, S., Atkins, L., & West, R. (2014). *The behaviour change wheel. A guide to designing interventions*, 1st edition. London: Silverback Publishing, 1003–1010.
Michie, S., Johnston, M., Abraham, C., Lawton, R., Parker, D., & Walker, A. (2005). Making psychological theory useful for implementing evidence based practice: a consensus approach. *BMJ Quality & Safety*, 14(1), 26–33.
Michie, S., Richardson, M., Johnston, M., Abraham, C., Francis, J., Hardeman, W., ... & Wood, C. E. (2013). The behavior change technique taxonomy (v1) of 93 hierarchically clustered techniques: building an international consensus for the reporting of behavior change interventions. *Annals of Behavioral Medicine*, 46(1), 81–95.
Michie, S., Van Stralen, M. M., & West, R. (2011). The behaviour change wheel: a new method for characterising and designing behaviour change interventions. *Implementation Science*, 6(1), 1–12.
Miller, W. R., & Rollnick, S. (2012). *Motivational interviewing: Helping people change*. New York: Guilford Press.
Moon, A., Carroll, S., Hudson, J., Hulme, K., & Moss-Morris, R. (submitted). Treating illness-related distress in people with physical long-term conditions: An evidence-based theory of adjustment to illness and treatment.
Moss-Morris, R. (2013). Adjusting to chronic illness: time for a unified theory. *British Journal of Health Psychology*, 18, 681–686.
NHS Health Scotland. (2019). Standards for the delivery of tier 2 and tier 3 weight management services for adults in Scotland. Retrieved from www.healthscotland.scot/media/2611/standards-for-the-delivery-of-tier-2-and-tier-3-weight-management-services-for-adults-in-scotland-english-oct2019.pdf (accessed on 1 April 2021).

Nueberger, J., & Tallis, R. (1999). Education and debate. Do we need a new word for patients? Let's do away with 'patients'. Commentary: Leave well alone. *BMJ*, 318(7200), 1756–1758.

Prochaska, J. O., & DiClemente, C. C. (1983). Stages and processes of self-change of smoking: toward an integrative model of change. *Journal of Consulting and Clinical Psychology*, 51(3), 390.

Prochaska, J. O., DiClemente, C. C., & Norcross, J. C. (1992). In search of the structure of change. In *Self change* (pp. 87–114). New York: Springer.

Roth, A. D., & Pilling, S. (2016). A competence framework for psychological interventions with people with persistent physical health problems. Retrieved from www.ucl.ac.uk/pals/sites/pals/files/migrated-files/Physical_Core_competences.pdf.

Segal, Z. V., Teasdale, J. D., & Williams, J. M. G. (2004). Mindfulness-based cognitive therapy: Theoretical rationale and empirical status. In S. C. Hayes, V. M. Follette, & M. M. Linehan (Eds.), *Mindfulness and acceptance: Expanding the cognitive-behavioral tradition* (pp. 45–65). New York: Guilford Press.

Scottish Government. (2018). *The delivery of psychological interventions in substance misuse services in Scotland*. Edinburgh: Scottish Government.

West, R. (2005). Time for a change: Putting the Transtheoretical (Stages of Change) Model to rest [Editorial]. *Addiction*, 100(8), 1036–1039.

Williams, C. J., & Garland, A. (2002). A cognitive behavioural therapy assessment model for use in everyday clinical practice. *Advances in Psychiatric Treatment*, 8, 172–179.

Afterword

Mark J. Forshaw

At this point, you will have read these remarkable stories behind the development of clinical practice in Health Psychology, as evidenced through these chapters, some more personal in focus, some more pragmatic and focused on delivery itself. Health Psychology is what Health Psychologists do, one might say. And, furthermore, Health Psychology clinical practice is what clinical practitioner Health Psychologists do. The beauty of these accounts is that they show what we all have in common, while also demonstrating the considerable diversity across individuals. I can see elements of commonality with my own clinical practice throughout these chapters, and I can learn from those who are doing things a little differently too.

For those who read this book looking for inspiration, I hope you found it. For those who wanted succour, and something to drive away a touch of imposter syndrome, I hope you discovered just that in these pages. Never forget that Health Psychology, like most healthcare disciplines, attracts what we call *agreeable people*. The thing about agreeable people is that they are *nice*, and they are not usually driven by ego (there are always a few exceptions, of course). They tend not to be pompous or self-important, and they respect others. Sounds great for a healthcare practitioner, doesn't it? It is. However, there is a downside: they are also more likely to berate and criticise themselves, and to lack confidence. This is why you will see imposter syndrome mentioned more than once in this volume; it's a real thing and most of us get that feeling sometimes. A lot of my life is spent supporting others through training, clinical supervision, and appraisals, to find ways to normalise and then minimise imposter syndrome so that it does not hold anyone back from achieving what they are capable of. In some ways, our obstacles to progress are often ourselves. The irony is that those of us who work clinically know that; we see it in the very clients we are trying to help.

The writers of the chapters in this book are some, but not all, of what I would call the pride of Health Psychology practitioners. I have worked or do work with most of them fairly closely, I am pleased to say, and others I have worked with more tangentially, some recently, some a decade or so ago. Health Psychology in the UK is still a family. It is no longer a cottage industry, we are beyond that, but it still *feels* like a family. This is what makes it easier for us to share ideas, in a relatively safe space, without fear or prejudice, and to learn from each other, accepting our foibles and sharing our successes. I would never want Health Psychology to stop feeling like that.

Index

acceptance and commitment therapy (ACT) 7, 22, 82, 100, 129–131
adjustment 49
antecedents-behaviours-consequences (ABC) model 124
anxiety 26, 46, 47, 83, 91, 94, 100, 131
assessment 98–113

behaviour change wheel 118
British Psychological Society (BPS) 4, 5, 43, 64, 70–71, 79, 95, 99, 108, 117

Cancer 42–56, 91
capability-opportunity-behaviour (COM-B) model 135–146
cardiac rehabilitation 63
clinical psychology
cognitive behaviour therapy (CBT) 7, 22, 24, 62, 79, 82, 99, 100, 103, 121, 124, 155
common sense model of illness representations 7, 8, 20, 131
communication 41
coping 45, 47, 48

decision making 51–53
dentistry (dental settings) 79–81
depression 46, 48, 83, 84, 131
diabetes 33–34, 35–36, 39, 60, 65, 67, 76–77, 83
distress 46, 48, 55, 91, 101, 105

empathy 103

five Ps model 124 et seq.

formulation 22, 46, 98, 117–155

Health and Care Professions Council (HCPC) 3, 5, 64, 71, 78, 79, 95, 98, 99, 110, 117

imposter syndrome 75, 159

leadership 28–29
long-term conditions 3–18, 34, 37, 87, 93, 98, 99, 110

mindfulness 7, 22
motivation-action-prompts model 118, 133–135
motivational interviewing (MI) 7, 22, 35, 100, 103

obesity 39, 40, 64–65
origami task 11–12

pain 19–29, 93
palliative care 35
patient-reported outcomes (PROs) 42, 53–54

quality of life 94

reflection 37, 54–55
research excellence framework 9
risk assessment 110–112

safeguarding – see risk assessment
self esteem 94
self harm 105, 110–112

162 Index

self-management 7, 25, 27, 34, 35, 37, 98, 99
smoking 34, 70
social cognitive theory 7
social cognitive transition, model of 49–51
stage theory 45
stress 23, 45, 47,105
suicidality 105, 110–112

teaching and training 26–28, 66–67, 95
theoretical domains framework 118, 121, 147
theory of planned behaviour 26
transdiagnostic model 131–133
transtheoretical model 150–151

weight management 39, 40

Printed in the United States
by Baker & Taylor Publisher Services